The Tunisian Exception

How Ancient Statehood And National Unity Shaped The Arab World's Most Cohesive Nation

GEW Social Sciences Group, Preface by Dr Hichem Karoui

Global East-West (London)

Copyright © 2025 by GEW Social Sciences Group

Preface by Dr Hichem Karoui

Collection: The Mediterranean Notebooks

Global East-West (London)

All rights reserved.

No portion of this book may be reproduced in any form without written permission from the publisher or author, except as permitted by copyright law.

Contents

Preface: The Carthage Foundation Debate ... 1

1. The Carthaginian Foundations ... 19
2. From Rome to Islam ... 31
3. Ottoman Autonomy and Pre-Colonial Statehood ... 49
4. Colonial Encounter and National Awakening ... 69
5. Building National Identity: Education, Memory, and Civic Consciousness ... 87
6. The Demography of Cohesion: Minorities, Integration, and Political Insignificance ... 107
7. Migration and State Capacity ... 127
8. Ideological Divisions Within National Unity ... 147
9. Regional Comparisons ... 167
10. The Future of Tunisian Exceptionalism ... 187

Preface: The Carthage Foundation Debate
Between Legend and New Genetic Evidence

By Dr Hichem Karoui

The traditional narrative regarding the establishment of Carthage focusses on Dido (sometimes referred to as Elissa), the Phoenician princess who purportedly escaped from Tyre in 814 BCE and constructed the "New City" (Qart Hadašt) along the North African coast of Tunisia. But groundbreaking genetic research published in 2025 has fundamentally challenged this story, showing that Carthage's population had very little genetic connection to the Phoenicians who are said to have founded it. This discovery has sparked a lot of scholarly debate about the city's true origins and the historical basis of the Dido legend.

The Story of the Old Foundation

The classical texts, especially Greek and Roman writers, present a fairly clear tale of how the world began. According to Justin's description of Pompeius Trogus, Dido ran away from Tyre after her brother Pygmalion killed her husband Sychaeus to obtain his money. When she went to the North African coast, she famously used the "Ox-Hide Trick."[1] She bargained for as much land as a bull's hide could cover, then cut it into small strips to make a much bigger area and build the fortress of Byrsa. [2]

The traditional foundation date of 814-813 BCE is derived from the Greek historian Timaeus of Tauromenium (about 345-250 BCE), whose chronology has been both validated and disputed by scholars. Archaeological evidence presents a more complex picture[3]: the initial residential levels at

Carthage have been dated to around 760 BCE, based on Greek Geometric pottery as a reference point. Nevertheless, radiocarbon analysis of faunal remains from excavations by the University of Ghent suggests dates at the end of the ninth century BCE. This places archaeological discoveries near the conventional literary date; however, it continues to provoke enquiries over the authenticity of the 814 BCE date as a historical fact or a post-event calculation.[4]

The Historical Accuracy of Dido: Academic Views

People still don't agree on whether Dido was a genuine person in the past. Books published hundreds of years after the establishment of Carthage contained the first references to her. The oldest person is Timaeus, who lived roughly 500 years after 814 BCE. Virgil penned the most famous version of the story in the Aeneid (around 31–19 BCE), where he made Dido Aeneas's contemporary and portrayed a tragic love story that took place more than three hundred years before Carthage was constructed.[5]

Contemporary scholarly discourse regarding Dido has significant fragmentation. Josephine Quinn from Oxford University has made a strong case that the Dido story, which was spread through Greek and Roman sources, is mostly a Carthaginian founding myth that the city told about itself, not just Greek or Roman propaganda. Quinn emphasises that the essential elements of the narrative, particularly Dido's rejection of the local Libyan monarch, Iarbas, and her subsequent self-immolation, correspond with the broader context of Carthaginian diplomacy and self-representation. Numerous scholars, ranging from Moscati in the 1970s to Quinn [6] in contemporary times, have contended that sufficient historical evidence substantiates the existence of Dido, while acknowledging mythological embellishments.

Several researchers, on the other side, conceive of Dido as a completely made-up person, like Romulus and Remus in Carthaginian history. Many historians don't think there is any historical validity to the story because all of the old records were written long after Carthage was founded, and the story has many made-up aspects.[7]

The Genetic Revolution of 2025: Carthage Without the Phoenicians

Nature published a thorough examination of ancient DNA in April 2025.[8] This was the largest threat to traditional storytelling. A group of researchers from around the world, led by Professor David Reich from Harvard University, Dr Harald Ringbauer from the Max Planck Institute for Evolutionary Anthropology, and Professor Ilan Gronau from Reichman University, looked at 210 genomes from people who were buried at 14 Phoenician and Punic archaeological sites across the Mediterranean, including Carthage itself. [9]

The findings were astonishing: during the period of Carthage's significance (6th to 2nd centuries BCE), its inhabitants had negligible genetic connections to Levantine Phoenicians. The study, on the other hand, found that most of the people who lived in Carthage were related to people who were genetically similar to ancient Greeks and Sicilians. There was also a smaller but growing group from North African groups. Dr Ringbauer observed, "Most people who were culturally Phoenician did not have Levantine ancestry." That was a big surprise and quite unexpected.[10]

The DNA studies indicated that the "Punic" groups were very different from each other. Most of the population in Carthage, which was supposed to be the centre of Western Phoenician civilisation, had European (Greek/Aegean and Sicilian) genetic profiles instead of Semitic ones. The North African genetic contribution was there and grew over time as Carthage's political strength grew, but it was still a minor part of the population at Carthaginian towns.[11]

The study documented remarkable genetic diversity and migration across the Punic domain. Researchers observed the burial of distant relatives in various parts of the empire. For example, they found two persons who were second or third cousins. One was from Kerkouane in Tunisia, and the other was from Birgi in Sicily. Researchers named this trend a "Mediterranean highway" of marine trade, which suggests that people were always travelling on it. [12]

Three Competing Narratives for Understanding the Genetic Evidence

The genetic discoveries from 2025 have led to three different ways of looking at them, each of which has important effects on how we comprehend where Carthage came from:

1. The "Cultural Franchise" Interpretation

The predominant scholarly perspective, posited by the study's authors, asserts that Carthage epitomised the inaugural biologically cosmopolitan civilisation—a cultural and theological "franchise" disseminated by the Phoenicians to nations lacking genetic affiliation. This hypothesis says that a small group of Phoenician settlers from Tyre started trading centres like Carthage, but they were quickly outnumbered by people from the area and other Mediterranean peoples, especially those from Sicily and Greece.[13]

This interpretation stresses that Phoenician settlements were mostly trading posts, with only a few Phoenicians living there. Many Phoenicians married individuals who were already residing in those areas. The Phoenicians' cultural supremacy, exemplified by their language, alphabet, and religious activities focused on Baal Hammon and Tanit, did not equate to population preeminence. Cultural identity was far stronger than genetic ancestry. The Carthaginians kept strong cultural ties to their Levantine ancestors, even though they had essentially little Levantine DNA.[14]

Professor Reich pointed out that this method is very different from how Greeks colonised at the same time. Greeks who fought Carthaginians in the Mediterranean "didn't mix much with local populations in the settlements they seeded." The Phoenician paradigm was wholly unique. It was more open, more cosmopolitan, and had a wider range of genetic diversity.[15]

2. The Indigenous Foundation Thesis

Some researchers and Amazigh (Berber) cultural activists support a more extreme view: that the genetic data shows that Carthage was not a Phoenician colony at all but rather an indigenous North African community that absorbed Phoenician civilisation. This viewpoint, promoted by the Amazigh World News and related outlets, asserts that Carthage and other cities designated as "Phoenician colonies" were, in reality, indigenous settlements—predominantly of Amazigh, Numidian, and Libyan origin—where Phoenician traders constituted but a small percentage.[16]

This interpretation corresponds with extensive Amazigh political and cultural activities that aim to contest perceived colonial narratives that obliterated indigenous presence and agency in North Africa. Supporters say they have been pushing this view for more than 35 years, and now DNA has proven what rigorous historical study has long suggested: Carthage was primarily a North African city based in the Amazigh and Numidian world.[17]

But this interpretation has many problems. The genetic data indicates that North African ancestry at Carthage and other Punic locations, although present, represented a minority component; the predominant genetic profile was Sicilian and Greek/Aegean, rather than indigenous North African. Furthermore, archaeological evidence indicates the absence of pre-Phoenician habitation at the Carthage site itself. Excavations at Bir Massouda and other sites have yielded no traces indicating prior habitation before the Phoenician arrival in the late 9th or early 8th century BCE.[18]

3. The Critique of the Methodology

A third position, put out by certain geneticists and historians, acknowledges the study's results but highlights substantial methodological constraints that hinder interpretation. Some important topics are[19]:

Time gaps: The study lacks genetic evidence from 900–600 BCE, the essential founding centuries of Carthage, as Phoenicians engaged in cremation prior to the 6th century BCE, rendering cremated bones incapable of providing DNA. All studied samples date from the 6th-2nd centuries BCE, centuries after the supposed founding date. Assertions on the genetic makeup of the initial founders are so tentative and possibly deceptive.[20]

Survivorship bias: The study exclusively sampled inhumed people, so favouring later groups that practised inhumation and potentially overlooking the genetic traces of earlier colonists who engaged in cremation. This bias prefers evidence of assimilation and hybridisation in later times, but it doesn't say anything about the founding population.[21] Critics say that "Levantine DNA" is too simple because it already had a lot of mixing by the Bronze Age, including Iranian/Caucasus and Steppe ancestries. Using "Levantine DNA" as a single category without identifying historical periods or regional differences makes it too simple, and it may not adequately show Tyrian genetic profiles from the 9th to 8th century BCE.

Limited sampling of founding sites: The study incorporated a limited number of samples from the initial occupation strata at significant sites, with numerous remains originating from earlier, inadequately documented excavations lacking clear context.[22]

These methodological issues indicate prudence in the interpretation of the results. One evaluation said, "The lack of earlier DNA samples leaves questions about when and how this genetic shift happened." There were probably not many Phoenician settlers at first, and their Levantine ancestry may have quickly faded via intermarriage, especially as Carthage flourished and Phoenician city-states in the Levant succumbed to empires like the Assyrians and Persians.[23]

The Archaeological Record: What the Ground Shows

To understand these varied points of view, you need archaeological information. Excavations at various sites validate that Carthage was founded as a Phoenician settlement in the late 9th or early 8th century BCE, with no indications of preceding Phoenician habitation at the site.

Bir Massouda, located in the heart of Carthage, has been the site of the most significant recent archaeological work. Excavations have uncovered large quantities of Phoenician and Punic artefacts that date back to the 8th century BCE. These discoveries clearly linked Phoenician ways of life to metalworking, city planning, and material culture. There have been no remnants recovered that show people lived there before the Phoenicians came.[24]

The Tophet of Carthage, a sacred site for Baal Hammon

and Tanit, is one of the oldest pieces of evidence indicating Phoenicians existed there. As part of a four-year effort from 2023 to 2025, archaeologists dug up many interesting things. They found nine gold coins from the 3rd century BCE (in 2023) and a 2,300-year-old marble mask of a woman with a Phoenician-style haircut (in November 2025). These artefacts support Carthage's Phoenician culture and demonstrate that the city was cosmopolitan, exhibiting a multitude of artistic and commercial influences.[25]

So far, attempts to date artefacts using radiocarbon have been made to connect the accepted date of 814 BCE with archaeological data. Early digs showed that people started living in the area around 760 BCE, but new radiocarbon tests on organic components from the first habitation strata have moved these dates back to the end of the 9th century BCE. This improvement makes the archaeological finds match up better with what is already known from books.

Trade, migration, and changes in the population over time

To understand how the number of people living at Carthage changed over time, you need to know about the larger networks of Phoenician trade and growth in the Mediterranean. Most Phoenician colonies had businesses that worked as trading posts rather than large-scale colonising efforts. The Phoenicians "didn't have enough people or need to build cities in other countries that could live on their own." There were fewer than 1,000 people residing in most cities.

Carthage and a few other villages eventually grew into big, autonomous cities, but the scenario wasn't the norm.

There were probably only a few dozen or a few Phoenicians living at Carthage at first. The founding traditions say that Libya, Berber people, and other Mediterranean civilisations had to help a lot with the quick rise. Historical documents show that Carthage had strong ties to the native people of North Africa. Initially, they paid homage to the local Berber tribes, but later they used treaties, trade agreements, and military force to take over the land.

By the early 4th century BCE, the Berbers constituted the largest part of the Carthaginian army. This shows that they are now part of Carthaginian civilisation. The "Libyo-Phoenician" societies mentioned in ancient texts—people who mixed Phoenician and Libyan cultural traits—are likely an example of this demographic trend.

The genetic data showing that most people in Carthage came from Sicily and Greece/Aegean suggests that migration from these places was far more important than anyone thought. Greek and Phoenician populations in Sicily were close, so people mixed easily. People from many different cultures arrived in Carthage to do commerce because Sicily and other Mediterranean islands became places where people could meet and share ideas.

The Dido Legend Revisited

How should we consider the Dido foundation myth now that we have DNA proof? You have three choices:

Rejection of historicity: The DNA evidence that shows

Carthaginians didn't come from Phoenicians can make the story of Dido seem completely false. How could a Tyrian princess have built Carthage if most of the people there weren't Phoenician? This view, on the other hand, mixes up stories about how a city was founded with data about its population hundreds of years later. Even if Dido or a small group of Tyrian exiles built the first town, their genes might have been lost in just a few years because of marriages and people moving in from other cultures.[26]

Myth with historical kernel: Josephine Quinn and others say that Virgil's romantic embellishment is clearly made up, but the basic account of Carthage is definitely based on real events. The city's name was Qart Hadašt, which means "New City." This means that it was built on purpose as a Phoenician foundation, not as an indigenous community. The enduring nature of Phoenician language, religious practices, governmental structures, and cultural identity throughout centuries indicates intentional transmission from a Phoenician founding population, regardless of genetic diversity or rapid intermingling within that society.[27]

Cultural memory rather than genetic history: The genomic data strongly shows that ancient identity was mostly based on culture, not biology. The Carthaginians preserved a Phoenician identity through the use of a Semitic language, the veneration of Canaanite deities, and the application of the Phoenician alphabet, despite possessing limited Levantine genetic heritage. The Dido mythology probably shows how the Carthaginians thought about and told the story of their origins. It created a basic myth that made their cultural ties to Tyre clearer while hiding the demographic differences in their real population.

Conclusion: Progressing Towards a Synthesis

The new DNA evidence has changed how we think about the inhabitants of Carthage, but it doesn't directly support the idea that "Carthage was not Phoenician" or that the city was built by North Africans who lived there. The data provides us a more complicated picture: Culturally, Carthage was Phoenician, but genetically it was completely unique. It started out as a little Phoenician trading port, but it quickly grew into a Mediterranean city with several various cultures. People arrived from North Africa, Greece, and Sicily.

There is no evidence that the Phoenicians lived at the site until 814–813 BCE, when they built a foundation there. The traditional story of how Carthage was established, which has some legendary parts, is probably based on what really happened when people from Tyre erected the city. It is not clear if a princess named Dido/Elissa led this voyage, but the story shows how the Carthaginians thought about their beginnings and kept in touch with their Phoenician roots.

DNA evidence shows that most of the people who lived at Carthage came from Sicily, Greece, and North Africa, not from the Levant. This population change happened even though the cultural identity was mostly Phoenician. This demonstrates that ancient Mediterranean cultures were founded on cultural identity rather than genetic identity.

The story of Dido is more than just a fable or a simple history. It is a cultural memory of how a very different set of people stayed connected to its founding story while simultaneously bringing in individuals from all around the Mediterranean. The "ox-hide trick" and sad love story may be legendary, but they hold a deeper truth: Carthage was really a "new city" that was built through migration, negotiation with native peoples, and the wonderful capacity to construct a unified cultural identity from quite different demographic sources.

***

For Further Reading:

Fantar, M'hamed Hassine Kerkouane A Punic town in the Berber region of Tamezrat, VI to Third century BC, Collection Mediterranean Heritage, 2007 Tunis.

Fantar, M'hamed Hassine Carthage Approche d'une civilisation, Tome I-II, Alif – Les éditions de la Méditerranée, 1998 Tunis.

Fantar, M'hamed Hassine Carthage, la cité punique, Alif, Les Éditions de la Méditerranée, CNRS Éditions, Paris, 1995.

Fantar, M'hamed H. in Presence Punique au Cap Bon (pp .51-94), Africa No. 5-6 1978.

Sources and References

1. Rose, Fiona. "Dido, Queen of Carthage | EBSCO." EBSCO Information Services, Inc. | www.ebsco.com, 2023. https://www.ebsco.com/research-starters/biography/dido-queen-carthage.

2. Fiona Rose, "Dido, Queen of Carthage | EBSCO," EBSCO Information Services, Inc. | www.ebsco.com, 2023, https://www.ebsco.com/research-starters/biography/dido-queen-carthage.

3. Nijboer, Albert, Karin Mansel, Boutheina Maraoui Telmini, and Fethi Chelbi. "NEW RADIOCARBON DATES from CARTHAGE: BRIDGING the GAP between HISTORY and ARCHAEOLOGY?" *Www.academia.edu*. Accessed July 15, 2024. https://www.academia.edu/28188258/NEW_RADIOCARBON_DATES_FROM_CARTHAGE_BRIDGING_THE_GAP_BETWEEN_HISTORY_AND_ARCHAEOLOGY.

4. Dridi, Hédi. "Early Carthage." Edited by Brian R. Doak and Carolina López-Ruiz. *The Oxford Handbook of the Phoenician and Punic Mediterranean*, August 12, 2019, 139–54. https://doi.org/10.1093/oxfordhb/9780190499341.013.11.

5. Phoenicians in Phoenicia. "Elissa (Dido) of Carthage in Legend & Myth," n.d. https://phoenician.org/elissa_dido_legend/.

6. Quinn, Josephine. "Prentice Lecture: Josephine Quinn." Princeton Classics, 2021. https://classics.princeton.edu/department/news/prentice-lecture-josephine-quinn.

7. Bbc.co.uk. "The Forum: Dido, Legendary Queen of Carthage," October 29, 2020. https://www.bbc.co.uk/mediacentre/proginfo/2020/43/the-forum-dido.

8. Callaway, Ewen. "Ancient DNA Reveals Phoenicians' Surprising Genetic Ancestry." *Nature*, April 23, 2025. https://doi.org/10.1038/d41586-025-01283-w.

9. Moeed, Abdul. "Carthage Was Not Mostly Phoenician, New DNA Research Reveals." Colombia One: News from Colombia and the World, April 24, 2025. https://colombiaone.com/2025/04/24/carthage-phoenician-dna/.

10. Curry, Andrew. "Most Phoenicians Did Not Come from the Land of Canaan, Challenging Historical Assumptions." AAAS *Articles DO Group*, April 23, 2025. https://doi.org/10.1126/science.z36xmn4.

11. in Carthage, The Archaeologist, April 27, 2025, Op.Cit.

12. Ibid.

13. Franz Lidz. "Who Founded Carthage? New Genetic Study Upturns Old View." *The New York Times*, April 24, 2025. https://www.nytimes.com/2025/04/24/science/archaeology-genetics-carthage-phoenician.html.

14. Exploreyourdna.com. "Phoenician Genes across the Sea: How Ancient DNA Reveals Their Mediterranean Legacy," 2025. https://www.exploreyourdna.com/article/58/phoenician-genes-across-the-sea-how-ancient-dna-reveals-their-mediterranean-legacy.htm.

15. The Archaeologist, April 27, 2025, Op, CIT.

16. News, Amazigh World. "Carthage Was Not Phoenician: Groundbreaking DNA Study Confirms Indigenous North African Roots | Amazigh World News." Amazigh World News, May 30, 2025. https://amazighworldnews.com/carthage-was-not-phoenician-groundbreaking-dna-study-confirms-indigenous-north-african-roots/.

17. Ibid.

18. Noerby Bonde, Bent. "Carthage Was Indeed Destroyed," n.d. https://www.media-progress.net/downloads/Carthage%20was%20indeed%20destroyed%20-%2021.3.2011.pdf.

19. Team, Editorial. "Evaluation of the Max Planck 210-Sample 2025 Phoenician Study - Let Africa Speak." Let Africa Speak, April 28, 2025. https://thinkafrica.net/max-planck-2025-phoenician-study/.

20. Ibid.

21. Editorial Team, Let Africa Speak, April 28, 2025, Op. CIT.

22. Ibid.

23. Giannopoulos, Bill. "Carthaginians Unraveled: Ancient DNA Shows Surprising Genetic Disconnect from Phoenician Roots." Greek City Times, April 25, 2025. https://greekcitytimes.com/2025/04/26/carthaginians-unraveled-ancient-dna-shows-surprising-genetic-disconnect-from-phoenician-roots/.

24. Academia.edu. "Carthage (Archaeology)," 2016. https://www.academia.edu/Documents/in/Carthage_Archaeology_/MostCited.

25. Bent Noerby Bonde, "Carthage Was Indeed Destroyed," Op. CIT.

26. Khan, Razib. "The Punic Paradox: Genetically, Rome's Great African Rival Was Startlingly European." Razibkhan.com. Razib Khan's Unsupervised Learning, June 12, 2025. https://www.razibkhan.com/p/the-punic-paradox-genetically-romes.

27. Sebastián Panatt. "Dido, Queen of Carthage." Substack.com. SP Historian , October 23, 2024. https://sebastianpanatt.substack.com/p/dido-queen-of-carthage.

1
The Carthaginian Foundations
Ancient Statehood and Institutional Continuity (9th Century BC – 146 BC)

Origins and Establishment of Carthage

The city-state of Carthage has continued to capture the imagination of historians, archaeologists, and amateurs alike with its history and basic origin. The founding myths and archaeological clues related to Carthage create compelling narratives that highlight differences in the governance of this civilisation. The Phoenician legend attributes the founding of Carthage to Queen Dido, also known as Elissa. She fled from the city of Tyre and is said to have greatly suffered while crossing the Mediterranean until she touched the northern part of the African continent, which was then the site of her new city. This marble tale is a testament to Phoenician culture and the benefits of the coastal city of Carthage. There have also been archaeological digs at Carthage, which have revealed traces of a settlement from the ninth century BC. At this point, the culture that made its home in this area is probably doing quite well. This research indicates that Carthage had worked out some form of governance and administrative control. This information paves the way for further investigation into the early history of the city.

Examining the history of Carthage more deeply, we realise that the merging of exploration, mythology, and societal change helped shape the onset and formation of the city. The Habana of Carthage and its legacy, and the Carthaginian history and myths, together tell us the full story of the Carthaginian civilisation.

> The more recent and credible academic resources offer a pointed critique of the Dido legend, focussing on it

and offering new interpretations about the foundation of Carthage. They argue that the city developed in a more complex and indigenous manner than as a pure Phoenician colonial outpost.

1. Genetic evidence suggests local and diverse origins

A study published in Nature and conducted by researchers at Harvard showed that ancient Carthaginians were genetically more similar to Greeks, North Africans, and Sicilians than to the Phoenicians from Tyre. Carthage and its surrounding settlements were the focus of the study, which involved specimens of the DNA of 17 individuals from Carthage and 86 individuals from its settlements. The findings indicate that Carthage was the result of considerable local and regional amalgamation, dominating the thought of a Phoenician-derived foundation population (Reich et al., 2025; The Archaeologist, 2025) (thearchaeologist.org).

2. Modern Scholarly Consensus on the Mythical Nature of Dido

The scholarly community, which consists of historians and archaeologists, has almost unanimously argued that Dido was a fictional character and not a real person. The earliest record of Dido comes from Timaeus of Tauromenium (3rd century BC), which is several centuries after the alleged foundation of Carthage; meanwhile, archaeological records indicate that settlement began in the middle of the 8th century BC, raising questions about the historical accuracy of Dido's life story (Mythosjourney, 2025; The Hellenica World, 2025) (mythosjourney.com).

3. Archaic myth as a cultural narrative rather than as a historical record

Some scholars venture that the founding myth—with

the legendary ox-hide trick—functions more as a cultural construct than as history. The ox-hide image, as one among many hundreds of numinous tales spanning Greater Eurasia, exhibits figurative imagination as storytelling rather than actual happenings. Concerning Carthage, it is probable that the story is mythologised rather than a historically accurate origin story (Oikonomidis, 2025) (archaeopresspublishing.com).

Political Structures and Governance

The political structures and governance of Carthage were deeply intertwined with the city-state's growing influence and power, having evolved into more than just a backbone to the Mediterranean. With the combination of various lands and cities that Carthage had influence and power over, the Carthaginian governance was layered around a bipartite system of political offices, councils, and ministers who managed intra- and inter-city matters. The highest office was with the suffetes, who kept state control with the support of the Council of Elders, made up of aristocrats and elected suffetes. The unity of free and active citizens complemented governance by backing state policies and giving authority to the popular assembly. The preserved form of governance in Carthage was more than influential, for it served to tackle the issues proposed by its society.

Additionally, Carthage's adoption of expansionist politics

and management of overseas territories contributed to the balance of its administrative system. The assignment of the judges' office as the governing body for the remote provinces in Carthage's dominions aimed to delegate power and ensure direct supervision; the decentralised structure governing each augmented dominion established a balance of power that supported both Carthaginian governance and local administration. Furthermore, Carthage's loyalty to its client kingdoms and alliances was crucial in supporting the construction of its geopolitical system within the surrounding maritime context.

The military's role in the governance system is just as important as the role of political institutions. The emergence of a professional army and a fleet protected the interests of Carthage and influenced policy-making. The administration of Carthage encompasses the distribution of military resources and the coordination of naval operations, illustrating the amalgamation of military might and policy in governance. Ancient Carthage's advanced governance structures and practices contributed to the city-state's rise to global power. The integration of political, administrative, and military governance is a testament to Carthaginian dynamism and statehood. Such approaches were impressively holistic, and they set a benchmark for future civilisations by demonstrating how their innovations influenced later cultures.

Economic Foundations and Trade Networks

Trade supported Carthage's economy and served as the foundation for its power. Because Carthage was located in the centre of the Mediterranean's trading network, it was able to trade by sea in many regions. Carthaginian ships maintained a powerful network of maritime trade, and the accumulation of resources helped the small state prosper. Carthaginian commerce penetrated far and beyond the Mediterranean. Trade encompassed the most economically dominating activities in the state and included metals, cotton, agricultural products, and exotic items. Carpets, along with the ever-elusive and highly sought-after ivory, were as prized as the spices that flavoured the various market regions. Mercantile policies directly facilitate the outreach of civilisations, in addition to the spillover of resources and the wealth generated by geography.

Carthage's economy was lively and diverse, featuring dynamic industrial growth and specialised industries with complex manufacturing techniques. Metalwork, shipbuilding, glassmaking, pottery, and other glassworks displayed the mastery of the city-state, solidifying the foundations of entrepreneurship and economic diversification. Though, the economic vitality of Carthage was sustained predominantly by the wealth from agriculture, enabling the hinterlands to grow grains and other staples such as olives, vines, and citrus for domestic purposes and for exports. The Carthaginian fleet primarily organised the trade routes, concentrating them centrally at Carthage's famous harbour among its other havens. Carthage's advanced port facilities played a crucial role in trade, allowing the city to store, transship, and redistribute cargo. Carthage also developed a strong and almost exclusive control over the colonies and trading posts that surrounded the city. These developments further supplemented Carthage's trade network and economic reach.

Carthage's urban opulence and advanced trade network fostered a cosmopolitan culture, transforming its diplomatic relations to a more international focus. This spread new ideas and thoughts, which fuelled the Carthaginian city-state's rich history of intellectual and artistic development.

The economic dynamism strengthened Carthage's position as one of the primary players in the ancient world and placed it in an advantageous position for further developments in trade, industrial activities, and cross-cultural interactions.

Military Innovations and Strategic Dominance

Innovations in warfare alongside the dominance exhibited during the reign of Carthage had long-lasting effects on history. Their reputation for being naval powerhouses stemmed from the advanced techniques developed by the Carthaginians in the construction of ships and naval warfare. The construction of quinquereme ships, featuring five stacked rows of oars, provided Carthaginian fleets with exceptional agility and swiftness, enabling them to dominate the Mediterranean. Furthermore, the innovation and Carthage's success in warfare were attributed to the deployment of unique weaponry, such as the lethal naval battering ram called a rostrum. Carthage was equally accomplished on land, with the conquest of the mercenary dominion of the Mediterranean providing it with a horde of troops and the proficient use of battalion war elephants, which served as psychological and physical weapons. The Carthaginian military head, Hannibal Barca, known for his strategic prowess, executed the tactics of the double envelopment in the battle of Cannae, illustrating confidence in the command and control abilities of the Carthaginian military. The vast diplomatic sphere of influence, which included numerous client states scattered around the Mediterranean, further enhanced Carthage's strategic dominance.

Carthage effectively controlled the trade routes and zones in the region, enabling it to leverage additional trade advantages and facilitate the flow of economic and military support, which ultimately allowed it to establish dominance over the Republic of Rome. This particular dominance enabled Carthage to become the leading power in the region, making it the target of all the other civilisations seeking control. In addition, the Carthaginians' ability to change and progress in the face of other growing civilisations and the military issues that surrounded them allowed Carthage to maintain its dominance. Their works of aid and those of other major towns, such as the protective Carthaginian walls, were strong military constructs that greatly aided Carthage's dominance in the region. Whenever warfare occurred, the remnants of Carthage were able to use their might and intelligence to maintain control, prolong conflicts, and support the infrastructure that contributed to their strategic efforts.

Subsequent generations inherited the military dominance resulting from Carthage's wealth. Following in its footsteps were the civilisations that emerged after Carthage itself.

Carthage's achievements inspired the great builders and masters of warfare we see today, as well as the authors of many great works.

Cultural Influences and Religious Practices

Ancient Carthage effectively used its established religion and culture to shape its ideology and governance.

The culture of Carthage was an amalgamation of various foreign influences, chiefly Phoenician, intercultural, and aboriginal. Religion was central to every aspect of life in Carthage: administrative, commercial, and social. The Carthaginians believed in numerous gods, of whom Baal Hammon and Tanit were the principal deities. Ritual sacrifice, particularly involving children, demonstrated a spirited religious commitment to the extent that such acts were commonplace. Scholars debated the prevalence and significance of child sacrifice in Carthaginian religion. Beyond religion, the fusion of Phoenician and indigenous elements profoundly reflected culture in art, architecture, language, and literature. The city's civilisation promoted artistic and intellectual pursuits, thus bestowing the region with substantial cultural assets. Moreover, the presence of different ethnicities, along with foreign influences, offered Carthaginian society an exuberant cross-cultural diversity. The society experienced a prosperous atmosphere, infused with a rich amalgamation of diverse cultures. The cultural influences of Carthage did, however, survive the centuries and reflect the traditions and rituals of the civilisations that came later and traversed the Mediterranean.

This diverse collection of cultures and heritage, along with the lasting historical influence of Carthage, demonstrates what it has contributed to history.

***

References For Further Reading

• Karapanagiotis, Ioannis. 2019. "A Review on the Archaeological Chemistry of Shellfish Purple." *Sustainability* 11 (13): 3595. https://doi.org/10.3390/su11133595.
A detailed review of physicochemical methods used to study Tyrian purple dye.
 • Metcalfe, Tom. 2025. "The Purple Dye That Powered the Ancient Phoenician Empire." *History.com*, June 11, 2025.
 Overview of the Phoenician monopoly on Tyrian purple and its economic and cultural significance. (history.com)
 • Rosa, Michele. n.d. *Delle Porpore e Delle Materie Vestiarie Presso Gli Antichi: Dissertazione Epistolare*. Moderna. (1786). John Crerar Library, University of Chicago.
 An early modern treatise on ancient purple dye and textile materials. (lib.uchicago.edu)
 • "Tyrian Purple: Rare, Valuable Dye from Greece's Bronze Age. Some History and Chemistry." 2024. *American Council on Science and Health*, June 26, 2024.
 Evidence of Bronze Age production of Tyrian purple at Aegina Kolonna. (acsh.org)
 • Iacovou, Maria, and Dimitra Mylona. 2019. "Pur-

ple Dye Production under Royal Management: Evidence from the Cypro-Classical Citadel of Ancient Paphos." *Cahiers du Centre d'Études Chypriotes* 49: 167–78. https://doi.org/10.4000/cchyp.586.

Archaeological findings of large-scale murex shell deposits indicating centralized dye production. (journals.openedition.org)

• Torr, Cecil. 1891. "The Harbours of Carthage." *The Classical Review* 5 (2): 189–200.

Seminal analysis of Carthage's cothon harbor infrastructure based on ancient sources and early archaeology.

• Lancel, Serge. 1995. *Carthage: A History*. Translated by Antonia Nevill. Oxford: Basil Blackwell.

2
From Rome to Islam
Institutional Layering and Cultural Synthesis (146 BC – 16th Century AD)

The Fall of Carthage and the Rise of Rome

The fall of Carthage shifted the balance of power in the Mediterranean by giving the Romans control of the country. The Romans were the victors of the Third Punic War, which took place between 149 and 146 BC. The lands that were taken over became part of the Roman provincial government. The territory went from being ruled by the Carthaginians to being ruled by the Romans. This transformed politics, society, and the economy all at once. Roman rule was established over the newly acquired Carthaginian territories, and the administration of the province was strengthened. The Romans administered provinces from the centre, which meant that there was the same level of authority in all of them, but people could choose how much power they wanted to have. Roman governors oversaw the provinces and could set imperial policy. They also provided some power to native leaders to run things. Consolidating power over the former Carthaginian kingdoms not only created a Roman-centred government, but it also made the local legal and financial systems the same across the board.

The Romans built new legal and economic systems in the countries they conquered, which were essentially Romanised. The integration process also helped the economy flourish since Rome spent a lot of money on building roads, aqueducts, public works, and other types of infrastructure. The rise of the additional places that were taken over also helped culture grow. During this time, Roman ethics, art, and culture were all very popular. Building new highways and establishing cities also made the artistic environment and society as a whole much better. The new Roman province's union with the ancient Carthage's territories brought new languages, customs, and ways of life to the Roman Empire. The Romanised provinces saw substantial changes in their civilisations, since they were a combination of Roman and native traditions. When Carthage fell and its lands became part of the Roman Empire, new cultural regions appeared. These were marked by more complicated administration and more advanced governing systems, as well as a time of cultural mixing.

There were many changes during Pasiphaë's administration of the Mediterranean expansion. These changes were caused by the conquests, the assimilations, and the new social and government systems that arose in the area.

The Roman Provincial Government and Local Freedom

After Carthage was conquered, the first changes were made to how the region was run and governed. The provinces were in control of the new territory, and each one had a prefect in charge. It was the job of the Circle Republics to collect and manage taxes and make sure that justice was served. The Republics of Rome were in charge of making sure that justice was served. The fundamental problems with Roman power over Carthage were the need for rational order and the need for independent, prescribed government. Their appropriate independence in local government helped keep

Indigenous local laws and regular cooperation. Roman rule made local governments stronger by establishing more rules, which made them stronger than any previous chief. Then, the chiefs took over the imperial system by taking control of local administration. Then, autonomy was important in the co-optation.

The Ottomans called areas that were officially ruled but still retained some Byzantine rule "border regions". There were a multitude of reasons for the Ottomans to construct additional provinces. It was also designed to improve the economy and order, just like it was meant to help culture thrive. The Ottomans were in command of the Byzantine region, but they sought to improve it socially and financially. The major purpose was to spread Byzantine culture through silks. A wider goal was to spread cultural assets all over the Ottoman Empire.

It was hard to identify where Byzantine culture ended and Ottoman culture began in this area. As cities in the Byzantine Empire strove to stay independent of the Ottoman Empire, streams of beautiful culture flowed in. These streams helped the Ottomans grow and spread their culture, which made the distinctions between the two cultures less evident. Both of them helped the economy and society. The Byzantine Empire had long since forgotten about the gems. Silks had been their main source of revenue for a long time. These streams of silk have got thicker and are now mixed with antique diamonds that tell the story of the empire. There are pop-up graphs all over the cities in the vicinity.

They wanted to improve civilisation, but the area tried to hinder the resources that helped the Ottomans flourish from flowing as much as possible. This stayed an inter-gem so that the people's needs may grow and find a new home in the gems of culture. The Byzantines perceived the same old thing as much less: the silk barrier where streams were lost. There was a patterned tapestry in Byzantine culture.

Changes in the economy during the time of the Romans

When the Romans took over Tunisia, it marked the beginning of a dramatic change in the region's economy. They revolutionised how trade and farming worked, and they even helped cities expand in the area. The Romans were responsible for Tunisia, while the economy and infrastructure grew considerably.

In the province, the Romans worked hard to develop roads, bridges, and ports. This made it much easier for people and goods to get about. These upgrades to Tunisia's infrastructure made trading inside Tunisia a lot easier, and trade with other parts of the Roman Empire even easier. Being part of the greater Mediterranean region helped trade in Tunisia and even with other parts of the Empire that were close by. Tunisia did quite well by selling olive oil, wheat, and other agricultural goods to other countries. The Romans also improved the government by making measurements the same and giving the region a unified currency. This gave the economy the stability it needed, which led to even more business. Colonising land, notably in the lush Cap Bon peninsula in the middle of the Empire and the capital of the province, made the area's food supply and farming much better. The Roman

Empire built cities like Carthage, Utica, and Dougga, which helped the administration, trade, and culture become more centralised.

Many various kinds of enterprises grew up in these huge cities because they drew both immigrants and skilled workers. The Roman upper class was particularly supportive of the arts and public works. These things added to the culture that was already there and made the area seem important. Even while Roman taxes were a hardship, they were utilised to protect the peace, create public buildings, and perform other things that were good for the city. This helped the economy of the region grow. The economic changes that took place during the Roman Period obviously made it easier for Tunisia to join the Mediterranean economy. The region's cities and businesses were affected by this for a long time after.

Cultural Exchanges and Romanisation

From 146 BC to the 16th century AD, cultural contacts and Romanisation changed the social and cultural fabric of the area. The Romans who conquered the native people made it hard for people from different cultures to get along. Both sides altered and took on pieces of the other side's culture. This cultural thread is what will set Tunisian culture apart from others. The Romans attempted to make the native people more like them by changing the laws, buildings, and customs and making Latin the main language of governance.

The Roman settlers and the people who already lived there blended their beliefs and ways of life to create a new and diverse civilisation. The Romans transformed the culture of these places by building big buildings in Dougga, Bulla Regia, and El Djem. The Romans created the roadways to protect and expand their empire and to make it simpler for trade to happen. But these roads were the major ways for culture, ideas, and religion to flow freely and mingle with those of the native people. The blending of religions and the uniting of gods with native followers led to the birth of a new, quite mixed-up religion. The Romans used complicated systems of irrigation and terracing that benefited the farming economy and productivity, which led to their success. Lastly, the spread of Roman philosophy and education led to the creation of an educated class that was familiar with Greco-Roman literature and philosophy. But the Romans had a bigger impact than the culture that prized money, philosophy, and study. A number of these cultural ceremonies were still going on alongside Roman ones. The fact that these two civilisations were so distinct from each other gave the area a lot of unique character.

The time of cultural exchange and Romanisation was a major aspect of the changes that would unfold in Tunisian history and identity.

The Rise of Christianity and Changes in Religion

Christianity developed in North Africa from the first to the fourth centuries AD, during the Roman and Byzantine periods. Christianity, as an emergent faith in the Levant, began its spread into the Roman province of Africa Proconsularis, undeniably affecting the region's cultural and religious norms. The shift from paganism to Christianity was a dramatic transformation in the views of individuals and society at large, influencing both religious and political sectors. Tertullian, Augustine of Hippo, and Cyprian were immensely significant in getting people in North Africa to become Christians. They worked hard to make Christian theology and doctrine easier for people to understand. During this time, big basilicas were built, new parts of the Church were made, and new kinds of Christian art were made. These developments were a sign of how the region's religious life was changing.

As the Christian community increased, it became harder to interact with the old Roman religions. This usually caused a long period of conflict and absorption. The bigger community stressed the time of Christian asceticism and monasticism, which was all on spiritual growth. This, together with the rest of society, helped make a large and lasting element of Christian devotion. The 4th century started with the exciting news that Emperor Constantine had become a Christian. This was also the first time an emperor acknowledged Christianity, which put an end to a time when Christians were being persecuted by the empire. Christianity entered a period characterised by financial support and expenditure, alongside the monopolisation of ecclesiastical privileges and theocratic rule. This made it easy for the first Council of Nicaea to get together in 325 AD. The goal of that meeting was to establish Christian truth and peace in doctrine. The blending of Christianity with its popularity in Roman jurisdictions led to a time of cooperation and conflict that defined the political and civic religious authority and practices at the community level. The history of Christianity in North Africa shows how different religions and civilisations can work together in a way that is both theologically advanced and politically active. It was a one-of-a-kind event that transformed how people thought about religion and theology in the area. Its active successors kept its memory alive for generations.

The Byzantine Empire's effects and modifications to the government

The 5th to 7th centuries were crucial in the history of the area because they saw changes in how things were administered and governed. The Byzantine Period was the most important one. It started with the fall of the Western Roman Empire and grew to include the northeastern parts of North Africa, such as what is now Tunisia. The Byzantine emperors transformed Tunisia's administration a lot by giving the central authority more power and making strict regulations about how people should live through Byzantine law. Byzantine administrative systems made the area more efficient and uniform by putting more focus on procedures than results. During the Byzantine period, Christianity grew, which helped construct social and institutional systems and led to the separation of religious and secular authority. The Byzantine model set up a system of secular government that worked well with Christianity. This made the administrative system more stable and peaceful. The Byzantine Empire also changed its legal practices because Emperor Justinian wrote down Roman law. Because there was no one person in charge of all the rules, the legal system had a lot of power over property, contracts, and civic duties. This made the judicial system more stable and easier to understand.

The Byzantines left behind a legacy that had a big impact on the creation and establishment of towns. This included erecting churches, public works, and defensive structures. These works from the Byzantine era are part of Tunisia's culture and history, which is why they are kept and studied. The Byzantine era in North Africa was challenging. There were invasions and wars within the region's own borders. Byzantine culture had a big effect on Tunisia's history and administration.

The early Islamic conquests and how they changed the area

The earliest Muslims to come to the Mediterranean and North Africa set the boundaries of those areas. The Rashidun Caliphate, a new Islamic faith, began to grow after the death of the prophet Muhammad in 632. Its disciples were the first to push its borders. The leaders of the Byzantine and Sasanian Empires gave the new religion to the people. Abu Bakr and Umar oversaw spreading Islam and the frontiers to the regions around the Byzantine and Sassanian.

The conquest of Egypt in 641 is significant, as it terminated Byzantine dominance in the region and initiated Arab governance and the proliferation of Islam. These changes not only impacted how the government worked in the area, but they also had a huge effect on social, economic, and demographic factors. The Islamic empire got stronger by taking over more land and areas. The empire got Islamic religion, legal systems, and administrative control from these new regions, which helped establish a new and very different

Islamic civilisation. The conquests also spread the Arab communal and tribal systems to other countries, which led to the rise of new political and social organisations. The Islamic conquest of North Africa, especially Carthage in 698, marked the end of Roman and Byzantine rule and the beginning of Islamic rule in the area. The Berber people in the area helped to improve Islamic culture, and in turn, Islamic civilisation made the Berber people better by combining cultures and languages. The Islamisation of North Africa was also crucial for influencing areas of culture, such as religion, art, and philosophy. It also caused substantial changes to physical structures like mosques and Islamic decorative arts.

The early Islamic conquests left behind many things that are still around today, like the use of Arabic, the observance of Islamic law, and even religious doctrines. Also, the fact that the society was made up of people from varied ethnic and religious origins helped develop groups that were open to different ideas. These things all led to the Islamic conquests, which had a huge effect on the civilisations in the area, especially in North Africa and the Mediterranean. These civilisations promoted extensive cultural contacts.

The Rise of Islam and the Rule of the Arabs

The arrival of Islam was one of the most important things that happened in Tunisia during Arab rule. It changed the history of the area in a big way. The Islamic Caliphate got a lot bigger in the 7th century because of Islamic conquests, such as the one in Tunisia. Along with the new faith, the Arab kings brought new ways of doing things and running things.

The Arab kings changed the economy, society, and culture in big ways. The introduction of Sharia law drastically changed moral and legal standards, changing the whole legal system and the values of society.

The Dominus Arabicus territory made Tunisia a place where religion and the Arabic language were particularly significant. This transition in history brought together and changed both Muslim Arabs and native Berbers, as well as those who had been Romanised. People from different civilisations came up with new, ingenious rituals with new patterns because they were inspired by the mix of cultures.

The new Tunisian identity was made up of parts from Berber, Roman, Arab, and Islamic traditions. It brought all of these things together to produce a unique Tunisian character, with a culture and manner of life that could only be found in that location. Tunisia's society became pluralistic by mixing Islam with many other religions and cultural traditions. The people who lived there had connections and ties that made this tolerance grow. Tunisia didn't suffer much because the Islamisation of the area began with a focus on converting Muslims. The new rule changed the culture of society by mixing Regia Arabica with indigenous building forms. The culture valued art and education, as shown by the founding of new schools. Many rationalists, philosophers, and theologians were drawn to this new form of arranging society, which was based on scholarship and inspired by the advanced and maintained schools of Islam. This concentration helped keep sophisticated works in philosophy, medicine, architecture, maths, and astronomy alive, as well as new ways of looking at astronomy.

When Arabs were in authority and Islam came to Tunisia, it was a highly critical moment for making Tunisian society more complicated and diversified. People from diverse cultures, religions, and races lived together peacefully in this civilisation. This time in history was the start of Tunisian civilisation, which combined old customs with the lasting effects of Islam in a unique way.

Cultural Synthesis and Diasporas

A lot happened in the world and in the area during this time. Islam expanded to Tunisia once the Arabs took power. This move sparked a complete shift in culture, with Byzantine, local, and new Islamic traditions mixing together in Tunisia. Also, the rise of these distinct cultural practices and traditions inside Islam has led to the formation of a new civilisation. The native and Islamic people were thrilled and celebrated this new culture, which was a sign of kindness and cultural diversity. All the different parts of society were connected to each other. Tunisia was a port city with people from many different cultures. It was located at the crossroads of various shipping routes across the Atlantic and Mediterranean. This made business expand. At that time, diasporas were particularly significant for moving goods and transmitting cultural ideas, beliefs, and practices all over Tunisia. Christianity and Judaism, along with their adherents, entered into agreements with Islamic civilisation that acknowledged and modified several of their practices. Because of this, there existed a close link between Islamic culture and Western culture. There were also new ideas, and culture grew throughout this time. Their literature, architecture, and music showed how well they worked together.

The mixing of different cultures made art that was more sophisticated and highlighted how different groups of people worked together. In addition, the new schools and research centres that sprang up became venues where individuals from all over the world could learn from each other and share ideas. Tunisia's culture and civilisation are still affected by this time period today. The impacts of cultural integration and diasporic links are still obvious and strong in the language, food, and customs that are now prevalent and seen as part of the national culture. The time spent promoting tolerance and diversity has strengthened social stability and unity in Tunisia, showing how cultural and regional integration may have an impact.

Socioeconomic Structures in Flux

During the time between Roman and Islamic rule in Tunisia, the area's social and economic institutions went through many changes that set the stage for future expansion. The new Arabian and Islamic rule in Tunisia caused modifications that contributed to the changes that happened when the Romans took over.

During the transition period, Arab leaders introduced new crops and irrigation technologies, which changed the way people farmed. These new ways of doing things, along with Islamic economic ideals, made trade thrive and market towns come to life. Islam also spread to the south. The growth of routes led to more trade and a broader network throughout the Islamic world, which helped the economy and culture grow. The transition period also saw changes in how land was divided and used. The new rulers of the area affected how people farmed by changing how land was divided and owned.

These changes brought in a new social and political order that was like the feudal system in some ways. They eventually used the money and political power they got to establish their social hierarchies. The new Islamic law and the financial Islamisation were the most important components of the economy and how public money was spent. The Islamic tax banking system provided funds that were used for construction, public works, and improving welfare programmes, which improved the overall well-being of the population. The emergence of novel community institutions transformed the region's demographic dynamics on a spiritual plane. The presence of Arab and Muslim settlers and the construction of Islamic institutions contributed to the ethnic and religious diversity. The resulting diversity led to a blend of new cultural practices that made the Tunisian identity even stronger.

During the transition period, Islamic architecture and other infrastructure improvements reshaped cities, both physically and socially. This was the origin of urban centres. When building Tunisia's cities, architects combined Roman and Byzantine styles with Islamic culture. They also paid close attention to new ideas and methods, as well as improvements in town planning and building design. Tunisia's economy and society changed a lot when it shifted from being ruled by the Romans to being ruled by Islam. This was a time when fresh ideas were really good. Tunisia's economy grew because agriculture, trade, and the legal and social systems all worked together. This made the country more culturally diversified. This became the most crucial part of Tunisia's past.

***

References For Further Reading

1. The Punic Wars and Roman Conquest of Carthage

Goldsworthy, Adrian. *The Fall of Carthage: The Punic Wars 265–146 BC*. Cassell, 2006.

Lancel, Serge. *Carthage: A History*. Translated by Antonia Nevill. Blackwell Publishing, 1995.

Warmington, B. H. *Carthage*. Robert Hale, 1960.

2. Roman Africa (General History, Economy, Society, and Culture)

Mattingly, David J. *An Imperial Possession: Britain in the Roman Empire, 43-409 AD*. Penguin Books, 2006.

Mattingly, David J. *Tripolitania*. University of Michigan Press, 1995.

Cherry, David. *Frontier and Society in Roman North Africa*. Oxford University Press, 1998.

Raven, Susan. *Rome in Africa*. 3rd ed. Routledge, 1993.

Whittaker, C. R. *Frontiers of the Roman Empire: A Social and Economic Study*. Johns Hopkins University Press, 1994.

3. Early Christianity in North Africa

Frend, W. H. C. *The Donatist Church: A Movement of Protest in Roman North Africa*. Oxford University Press, 1952.
Tilley, Maureen A. *The Bible in Christian North Africa: The Donatist World*. Fortress Press, 1997.
Brown, Peter. *Augustine of Hippo: A Biography*. University of California Press, 2000.
Barnes, Timothy D. *Tertullian: A Historical and Literary Study*. Oxford University Press, 1971.

4. Byzantine Rule in North Africa

Diehl, Charles. *L'Afrique byzantine: Histoire de la domination byzantine en Afrique (533-709)*. Ernest Leroux, 1896. (Classic, though dated, comprehensive work)
Cameron, Averil. *The Mediterranean World in Late Antiquity, AD 395-600*. Routledge, 1993.
Procopius. *History of the Wars, Books III and IV (The Vandalic War)*. Translated by H. B. Dewing. Harvard University Press, 1916-1940 (Loeb Classical Library).

5. Early Islamic Conquests and Arab Rule in North Africa

Brett, Michael. *Islam and Colonialism: Western Perspectives on North Africa: A Handbook of Historical Sources*. Routledge, 2014.

Brett, Michael. *The Rise of the Fatimids: The World of the Mediterranean and the Middle East in the Fourth Century of the Hijra, Tenth Century CE*. Brill, 2001.

Hrbek, Ivan (ed.). *General History of Africa, Vol. III: Africa from the Seventh to the Eleventh Century*. UNESCO, 1992.

Kennedy, Hugh. *The Great Arab Conquests: How the Spread of Islam Changed the World We Live In*. Da Capo Press, 2007.

Abun-Nasr, Jamil M. *A History of the Maghrib in the Islamic Period*. Cambridge University Press, 1987.

6. Cultural Synthesis and Socioeconomic Structures in Flux

Braudel, Fernand. *The Mediterranean and the Mediterranean World in the Age of Philip II*. Translated by Siân Reynolds. University of California Press, 1995.

Lapidus, Ira M. *A History of Islamic Societies*. 3rd ed. Cambridge University Press, 2014.

Savage, Elizabeth (ed.). *The Human Commodity: Perspectives on the Trans-Saharan Slave Trade*. Frank Cass, 1992.

3
Ottoman Autonomy and Pre-Colonial Statehood
(1574–1881)

Historical Context and the Rise of Ottoman Influence

Regarding North Africa, the expansion of the Ottoman Empire was the first step of great historical importance to the area and came with many intricate political and strategic goals. During the sixteenth century, the Ottoman Empire was attempting to expand its rule, moving beyond Anatolia and the Balkans to the richly endowed North African regions. This mission was driven by Ottoman ambitions to control important routes, gain valuable resources, and influence trade in North Africa. They also aimed to counterbalance the dominance of other European powers and maintain control over crucial waterways. What was also important was that the Empire needed to establish forward bases to support its Mediterranean operations, enabling the projection of power and protecting its trade. The regions of present-day Tunisia, Algeria and Libya that came under Ottoman control altered the political structure of the area. It was the first step to establish the administrative and internal control needed to maintain external Ottoman administrative efficiency.

Through control of alliances with some indigenous elites and various tribal units, the Ottomans exercised their power over the territory with control and ease, all the while keeping the stability and complications of governance overlooked. During this period, a peculiar blend of indigenous and Ottoman governing techniques developed, significantly influencing the area's socio-political issues. Moreover, the expansion of the Ottoman Empire into North Africa had other far-reaching effects with respect to the exchange and integration of cultures. The arrival of the Ottomans, along with their customs and traditions, brought about interaction with the local customs, languages, and even beliefs, resulting in a complex net of cultural relationships. The impact of the interaction between the indigenous culture and the ensuing Ottoman Empire influenced even the cultural aspects of North Africa and changed its identity and heritage. The culture in Africa, with varied elements that dominated during the Ottoman period, also substantially influenced the other regions under the Ottoman Empire, in addition to enhancing the artistic as well as architectural scholarship of the area and the flow of ideas. The case of North Africa is not as simple as it may seem; to some, it is a rich narrative illustrating the practical use of political ambition, along with other Ottoman strategic elements, coupled with adaptive governance and dexterous handling of the synthesis of cultures.

Analysing the relationships the Ottoman Empire had with the native populations in the region, is important because of the legacy that this unit of study provides, as well as the importance placed on the events that followed in North African history.

Structures of Governance: Autonomy Under Ottoman Rule

Besides autonomy in the Empire as a whole, the rule of the Bey, the province's governor, was still able to maintain custom and order in Tunisia, collecting taxes for the Ottomans. This type of autonomy allowed for significant local governance, as the Bey only required the "head of the provincial administration" to respond to his orders. Compared to the rest of the Empire's legal and administrative constructs, Tunisia was able to maintain its own. Along with the local officials he was able to appoint and the constant control he had over both local commerce and trade, the Bey's powers seemed absolute. Autonomy of this specific type was derived from a mixture of social and political relations aimed at Ottoman influence, as well as the continuity of native power.

The Ottoman rule and autonomous governance touched on the impact of cultural and religious practices in Tunisia. Maintaining the customs of the region, the Ottoman rulers were passionate about maintaining control over the province. Their approach minimised the diluted Tunisian identity and heritage within the imperial scope. Autonomy rule during the Ottoman period cultivated a spirit of Tunisian resilience and adaptability. Local leaders, along with elites, were vital in managing the daily activities of the population and meeting their needs. As leaders, they often advocated with Ottoman representatives for the protection of the province's interests. Their advocacy with Ottoman rule progressively strengthened autonomy and allowed for a certain level of self-governance in internal regulation and economic control. Their advocacy with Ottoman rule progressively strengthened autonomy and permitted a certain level of self-governance in internal regulation and economic control. Tunisia's enhanced autonomy resulted in distinct socio-political structures within the country. Local councils, religious bodies, and tribal affiliations significantly impacted governance processes. Ottoman rule and control, along with the self-made power structures of Tunisia and the soft power balance they provided, gave this area a distinct and uncommon type of governance for over 100 years. Tunisian colonial rule during the Ottoman reign had a significant impact.

The governance structures of the Ottoman period demonstrate a balance of power and decentralisation of authority concerning the complexity of an empire's rule and the survival of domestic systems beyond the influence of foreign elements.

Socio-Political Dynamics and Indigenous Elites

The period of Ottoman autonomy in Tunisia was marked by complex socio-political interactions between local elites and the Ottoman overlords. Within the region, the indigenous elite class, consisting of influential tribal leaders, wealthy landowners, and local administrators, were pivotal in the maintenance of order and stability. As intermediaries between the provincial Ottoman government and the population, they exercised a lot of influence and power. Their collaboration with the Ottomans facilitated the retention of traditional sociopolitical structures and governance, thus providing a semblance of stability in the face of external political upheaval. Nevertheless, the local elites had to balance the complexities of shifting political tides, where they had to prove their loyalty to the Ottoman Empire while still pursuing their self-interest and autonomy. These fragile socio-political balances frequently led to complex power struggles and negotiations that characterised Tunisia's pre-colonial sociopolitical landscape. This local elite class also enhanced the economic prosperity and cultural development in the region. Their patronage of the arts, literature, and architecture contributed to the cultural development of society, and the legacy of intellectual and creative Tunisia is still evident today.

The indigenous elites faced challenges as a result of their status. The emerging bureaucratic structures and centralised authorities scrutinised internal and external pressures within the Ottoman Empire more closely. Disparities in power and control among the Ottomans hindered the initial stages of significant changes in Tunisia's socio-political structure. The next evolutionary theories will address these changes and their effects on Tunisia's political and historical relations and its national and state development.

The Role of Trade and Economic Transformations

The period of Ottoman independence in Tunisia was marked by radical changes in trade and other economic activities. They were crucial in shaping and changing the region's political and social landscape. Tunis was then strategically positioned as a centre for Mediterranean trade. In those days, Tunisia was strategically positioned and central to Mediterranean trade. The merging of Europe, Asia, and Africa brought a shower of products that diversified the commercial activities of Tunisia. Consequently, there were vibrant centres of commerce and artisanal production. Tunisian merchants established complex trade routes that connected them to people in distant countries.

The Ottomans, along with other rulers, expanded and modernised their economies, which included agriculture. There were innovations with irrigation and crop growing that increased the productivity of farms and cash crops such as olives, wheat, and barley, which were grown not only to satisfy domestic needs but also to serve as trade commodities for other bordering states and even for European powers. There was also the development of agricultural trade on a larger scale, which greatly economically connected the Ottoman Empire to markets beyond the Mediterranean.

The period of the Ottomans, apart from military and naval strengths, also expanded their integration and connections with the financial Silk Roads. The development of financial networks and integration with the Silk Roads facilitated the flow of credit, currency, and regulated investment mechanisms, which not only opened new borders of trade but also strengthened local financial institutions and financial trade partnerships, which fostered entrepreneurial growth. The foldable Ottoman trade empire also bolstered the development of trade in the Mediterranean, and new advances in naval and shipbuilding boosted trade beyond the Mediterranean. The new economic and social changes led to a shift in the Empire's class structure, creating a powerful merchant and trade elite, while new Ottoman urban centres emerged, transforming the old culture into a cosmopolitan urban one and fostering new societal norms.

To conclude, the Tunisian provinces of the Ottoman Empire enjoyed autonomy for many years, and during this time, Tunisia underwent extreme economic change due to the province's becoming a major centre of Mediterranean trade. This economic growth allowed Tunisia to gain new levels of sophistication in commerce, agriculture, and finance, which shaped the country's economic and societal structures, in turn strengthening the region.

Cultural Influences and Institutional Developments

Cultural influences and institution building helped guide Ottoman autonomy along with pre-colonial statehood in Tunisia between the years 1574 and 1881. The region was deeply affected by various interrelated cultural streams: indigenous, Ottoman, and Mediterranean. Here, we focus on the spatial manifestations of cultural interactions and the resulting cultural institution building.

The blending of Islamic, Arab, Berber, and Ottoman cultural influences created a unique set of traditions, customs, and social practices. Such cultural influences were particularly visible in the form of governance and administration, which resulted in the intermingling of local indigenous customs with Ottoman institutional frameworks.

In addition to art, architecture and language features contributed to the development of a distinct Tunisian cultural identity that set it apart from the rest of the Ottoman Empire. The impact of these cultural contacts extends to various fields, including law and education, exemplified by the combination of Islamic law and traditional Ottoman law. The blending of these interconnected cultures created a legal system that mirrored the characteristics of mixed cultures. This framework served as a foundation for governance and justice, giving a reflection of the mixed cultures.

Military Affairs – Local Armies and Defensive Strategies

During the period of autonomy for the Ottomans and the pre-colonial statehood of Tunisia, the military's mosaics were complex, including local armies and defence systems to protect the region. Indigenous people and foreign mercenaries formed the local armies. The Ottomans used local armies constructed of many ethnicities and religions to aid in the defence of the internal and external borders. The Ottomans relied on the unique and diverse ethnic and religious groups because of their superior terrain and tactical warfare knowledge. They knew how to protect Ottoman interests in Northern Africa. The defence strategies employed during that period included various enhancements. They had advanced fortifications. The defence strategies included both coastal defensive measures and advanced naval warfare techniques. The relative position of the chains of forts along the main sea routes, as well as the timber that serves as the principal defensive chains at sea, indicates the importance of securing access to the sea. The defensive measures taken were intended to protect the region and maintain its economic importance.

In addition, the military apparatus was part of the greater power structure of the Ottoman Empire, which systemically balanced central authority and local freedom. The consolidation of military operations, logistics, and provisioning was integrated not only into governance but also into the intricate administrative capabilities of the elite. The shifting geopolitical context of Europe and growing colonial interests necessitated a significant evolution in the forms and methods of defence. The pressures from European powers on the empire's borders warranted further introspection on its defences, ultimately leading to the modernisation of military and infrastructural genius and the application of rest tactics. The synthesis of local armies, defence strategies, and socio-political relationship shifts captures the complex character of military operations in the Ottoman autonomy epoch. Grasping the delicacy of relations, competitions, and strategical needs harks back to the military history of Tunisia and the profoundness of relations and independence's enduring impacts.

Jurisdictional Systems and Legal Traditions

During the Ottoman autonomy period, significant advancements were made in jurisdictional systems and legal traditions in Tunisia. The period represented a strong conglomerate of local legal practices and the adoption of Ottoman legal systems.

The Ottomans instigated their form of legal structure. However, in many parts of Tunisia, customary law still dominated. A notable feature of that era was the presence of significant legal pluralism. While Islamic law served as the cornerstone of the legal system, indigenous conflict resolution methods and social customs played a crucial role in resolving local matters. The resulting dualism gave rise to a complex legal system. There were legal traditions where the customary law and the religious law coexisted and, in some cases, were in conflict. Additionally, the Ottoman rulers established a hierarchical system of courts to dispense justice and maintain control. The religious courts deal with civil and criminal cases, while the Sharia courts deal with family and religious issues. Such a system of legal subdivisions formed a legal mosaic characteristic of Tunisia before colonial domination. The Ottoman era marked a significant milestone in the systematisation and writing of legal norms. The collection of legal documents and texts aimed to unify legal practice and standardise the interpretation of laws.

One positive outcome is that documented legal norms and precedents formalised legal traditions in the Tunisian context and progressively reconstructed the legal framework. The legal traditions that emerged during the period of Ottoman Autonomy also showed the impact of Islamic law and the Maliki school. The progressive Islamic law alongside local legal systems indicated the active legal climate Tunisia was experiencing then. These legal traditions and instruments determined not only the legal systems but also the socio-political systems of Tunisia.

In short, during the period of Ottoman Autonomy in Tunisia, numerous legal traditions and jurisdictional systems emerged, the dominant features of which were Islamic law, local traditions, and the Ottoman legal system. The fusion of these elements created a complex legal system that served as the foundation for the development of future legal systems. The value of these legal traditions serves to illustrate the complexity of Tunisian justice in the pre-colonial period, which outlines the framework for understanding the traditions of Tunisian law that have survived until our time.

Social Hierarchies and Class Structures

Ottoman Era Tunisia was a society with many layers of hierarchies and class systems, which influenced the social dynamics of the country.

The ruling class that sat at the uppermost part of the social hierarchy included Ottoman officials and local elites who held powers of considerable authority. The social and economic... In this complex social order, the wealth and privileged lineage of the ruling class enabled them to claim 'social' and 'public' honours, placing them at the apex of society alongside upper-class aristocrats, landowners, and prominent merchants. They were completely unaware of the social structure that their successors adhered to. Craftsmen and peasant labourers comprised the lowest tier of this disrespectful social order. Instead, the lower segments found themselves deeply enmeshed in the harsh silence of blame and self-denial as they endured malnutrition and mistreatment. In Tunisia, a social order existed that included hierarchies defined by 'ethnic' and 'religious' characteristics, which determined how inclusive or exclusive each layer of society was for its members. The interaction of various Arabs, Berbers, Jews, and Christians with different religions and cultures led to a complex relationship with the social order of Tunisia, in which the new Tunisians were being colonised.

In addition, the roles of gender and family relations were crucial in the preservation of social stratification, as the patriarchal system and family ties helped sustain the ancient systems of social and political domination. Within the above social systems, some individuals tried to change the social order from within by using education, business, and social activism. These activities created social change and some social tension in the old class systems by transforming the class structure and the static societal order. Explorations of social order and class systems address the history of stratification in Tunisia, revealing the old Tunisia's sophistication of social structure, the distribution of power, and the lived realities of many different social classes. The fine details of social stratification involve Tunisia's history; thus, the study of social stratification provides context for Tunisia's history, structure, and systems of domination.

Challenges to authority: revolts and rebellions

The Ottoman Autonomy in Tunisia experienced several challenges to its authority for centuries as society and politics became infused and increasingly intertwined with revolts and rebellions. These challenges to the Ottomans involved factors such as the economy, unequal social classes, and a lack of self-governance, most likely originating from foreign dominance. This phenomenon was likely due to the presence of discontent among peasants, who sided with urban labourers as their methodologies contested those of the Ottoman rulers. Additionally, many tribal and region-specific social tensions compounded social eruptions, civil disobedience, and defiance. These social outbursts of fury and rage began to become more coherent, organised, and coordinated, resulting in widespread uprisings. Not only did these forms of resistance aim to contest power, but they also sought to strengthen self-alternative governance and a sophisticated order within society.

Primarily due to the indomitable forces of revolts and rebellions, mechanisms were put in place to establish power over religious and cultural self-governance, as the natives rejected most external forces linked to their self-identity and way of life. Many alternative leaders and ideological movements overshadowed the predominance of the established social order, as the leaders of authority were challenged. Within these movements, many questioned the validity of the ruling elite and proposed alternative governance systems that resonated with the people's aspirations.

However, these movements were not restricted to political authority alone; they often encompassed a broad range of self-definition and self-governance actions. The Ottoman Empire itself faced numerous revolts and rebellions that were countered, more often than not, with a combination of overwhelming military force, subtle diplomacy, carefully constructed alliances, and skilful bargaining to quell unrest and maintain some semblance of authority. The strength and resilience of the opposition, however, indicated a profound layer of challenges and difficulties tied to governing a multi-faceted and fluid society. All these revolts and rebellions that occurred during this time period had a significant influence on Tunisian pre-colonial history, as they set the stage for developments concerning statehood, nationalism, and the struggle against colonial rule.

Emergence of Pre-Colonial Nationhood and Identity

The emergence of pre-colonial nationhood and identity within the context of statehood and Ottoman autonomy had a considerable influence on history within the region. The decline of power within the Ottoman Empire gave rise to the assertion of identity and the claim to a distinct sense of nationhood by local communities and indigenous elites. The region's pre-colonial statehood and Ottoman autonomy were, however, not devoid of pre-colonial and colonial influences. The interplay of these activities was the product of a multitude of elements, factors, and influences, some of which were cultural, social, political, and economic.

The articulation of linguistic and cultural identities was one of the salient features of this emergence. Isolationist communities began to adopt local languages and customs, constituting an external 'other'. This cultural reaffirmation imbued the greater public with a new sense of cohesiveness and common ancestry as the first step in the formulation of nationhood. Furthermore, borderless trade and networked economic activity also contributed to diminishing the developing sociocultural matrix of emerging nationhood.

The circulation of tradeable goods and idea exchange linked isolated communities and regions, laying the groundwork for shared commercial customs and economic symbiosis. These activities positively reinforced collective feelings of nationhood among all the constituent units of the emerging nation. Ultimately, the simultaneous development of all these features prompted indigenous elites to lead the social and political mobilisation of their communities, along with the expression of a predominantly popular imagination. These elites, patrons of cultural and intellectual activities, employed the united local traditions to create a political purpose defined by a new imaginary filled with shared history and destiny. Regional mythologies transcending local borders and the traditions and histories that were their core were creatively synthesised.

The perception of identity in the precolonial period was, in part, a reaction to both outside control and domination, and the emergence of nationhood in the territory was intertwined with these expansionist and colonising duels to access the region's resources. As European colonialists competed for control of the area, people sprang to defend themselves by upholding common symbols and myths of the people. The latter part of these developments satisfied the 'centring of political power' thesis and identity formation, which resonates with the idea of Tunisian nationalism. The development of pre-colonial identity and nationhood, as a result of the multifaceted developments, became the first markers in Tunisian anti-colonial discourse. Most importantly, they enabled the formation of identity and memory, which in turn continues to shape the modern perception of Tunisia.

***

⊠References For Further Reading

In Arabic

Ahmed ibn Abi Dhiaf: Ethafu Ahl-i-ZZaman bi Akhbari Tunis wa 'Ahdi-l- Aman. [Entertaining the People of the Time With News from Tunisia and the Era of Security]. Al-Dar al-Tunisiyya Lil-Nashr (Tunisian Publishing House). Tunis, 1989. (8 volumes).

Foundational & General Histories

1. Abun-Nasr, Jamil M. *A History of the Maghrib in the Islamic Period*. Cambridge University Press, 1987.
2. Julien, Charles-André. History of North Africa: From the Arab Conquest to 1830*. Edited by C.C. Stewart, Praeger, 1970.
3. Laroui, Abdallah.The History of the Maghrib: An Interpretive Essay. Princeton University Press, 1977.

Governance, Autonomy, and the Beylical State

4. Brown, L. Carl. The Tunisia of Ahmad Bey, 1837-1855. Princeton University Press, 1974.
5. Cherif, Mohamed-Hédi. Pouvoir et société dans la Tunisie de Husayn bin Ali (1705-1740). 2 vols., Université de

Tunis, 1986.

6. Mantran, Robert. "La Régence de Tunis au XVIIème Siècle." Cahiers de Tunisie, vol. 12, 1956, pp. 1-20.

Socio-Economic & Cultural History

7. Valensi, Lucette. On the Eve of Colonialism: North Africa before the French Conquest. Africana Publishing Company, 1977.

8. Clancy-Smith, Julia. Mediterraneans: North Africa and Europe in an Age of Migration, c. 1800-1900. University of California Press, 2011.

9. Larguèche, Abdelhamid. Les Ombres de la Ville: Pauvres, Marginaux et Minoritaires à Tunis (XVIIIème et XIXème Siècles). Faculté des Sciences Humaines et Sociales de Tunis, 1999.

Military, Legal, and Institutional History

10. Toumi, Mohsen. La Tunisie ottomane: institutions militaires et société (XVIe-XVIIIe siècles). Nirvana, 2014.

11. Ze'evi, Dror. An Ottoman Century: The District of Jerusalem in the 1600s. State University of New York Press, 1996.

12. Çizakça, Murat. A Comparative Evolution of Business Partnerships: The Islamic World and Europe, with Specific Reference to the Ottoman Archives. Brill, 1996.

Revolts, Identity, and the Path to the Protectorate

13. Perkins, Kenneth J. A History of Modern Tunisia. 2nd ed., Cambridge University Press, 2014.

14. Green, Arnold H. The Tunisian Ulama, 1873-1915: Social Structure and Response to Ideological Currents. Brill, 1978.

4
Colonial Encounter and National Awakening
(1881–1956)

The Effects of Colonial Dynamics

The early stages of colonialism in Tunisia were important events in history. Different social groups reacted to colonisation in different ways. The native Tunisians were made up of Arabs, Berbers, and other ethnic groupings. Some Tunisians didn't like the French and didn't care about them. People thought the French were harmful for the economy and society because they seized land and used people. The French created administrative systems in Tunisia to protect it, which revealed how their colonialism was rude and dehumanising. The residents in the region kept complaining more and more. People also didn't pay attention to their fears that the social and political authorities would take over. Responses to the new political dynamics focused on social and political powers, which were based on the social and economic systems of colonialism. The new rules make it apparent how to get around in society, how to get involved in politics, and how to be politically and civically active.

Colonisation also had an impact on the Jewish community. Colonisation affected the Jewish community's sense of self, leading to questions such as "Who am I?" "Where do I fit in?" and "Is my life worth living?" 'and 'Is my life worth living? There are also concerns of loyalty that can make people react quite differently and strongly, depending on where they are and what class they are in. Responses to colonialism in different areas showed a complex web of relationships that were shaped by social, personal, historical, and future factors.

The analysis of reactions during this initial period provides insights into the dynamics between the coloniser and the colonised, framed within the socioeconomic framework of Tunisia, thereby laying the groundwork for subsequent societal discontent and emerging patterns of resistance.

The Creation of the French Protectorate

The French Protectorate in Tunisia was a critical event in history that changed the country's politics, society, and economy in a large way. The Treaty of Bardo made Tunisia a French protectorate in 1881. The treaty took away almost all of the Husainid Bey's power and control over military, financial, and foreign affairs, turning him into a puppet of the French colonial government. Tunisia's political history changed.

The creation of the protectorate brought about major changes in many areas of Tunisian life. The French transformed Tunis's farming economy by emphasising exporting cash crops and natural resources. This plan led to the rise of commercial farming on huge amounts of land, which took away land from Tunisians and left many of them destitute. Also, unfair French trade policies made things worse by hurting local businesses and boosting French businesses, which made the gap between the two economies even wider. The French Protectorate was the first step in Tunisia's social and cultural integration into French rule. The French language and culture were given more priority, and the school system was altered to fit French standards, which pushed Tunisia's local legacy to the side. The purpose of taking away Tunisia's native knowledge was to make Tunisians feel awful about their culture and history. The protectorate's political control meant that the colonial government had all the power, which meant that Tunisians had no meaningful voice in how things were run. The French government assumed control of the administrative machinery that was supposed to keep colonial rule running smoothly. There was no more local self-government.

Tunisians were getting angrier with the foreign authorities because they felt that they were losing control over their own lives. When the French Protectorate started, Tunisia's route to finding its own identity and making its own decisions shifted. The ramifications of this epoch on Tunisia's history would continue for decades. It would also lay the framework for Tunisia's first nationalist movements for independence.

Changes in the economy during the time of colonial control

The French began to colonise Tunisia in 1881, and the country's economy began to change. Tunisia began to restructure its economy, which had effects on the country that lasted for many years. The French colonisers transformed Tunisia's economy and began farming on a large scale for themselves. People used to consume crops, but now they eat wheat, olives, and grapes. This change impacted families in the country, and the rich landowners ended up with more money and land than they needed. People were also more upset with each other after this change. The French colonisers accelerated the process of taking minerals and phosphates from Tunisia to help Europe become more industrialised. This damaged Tunisia and primarily aided France's economy. This industrial economic exploitation generated problems for the people of Tunisia, who were colonised, both socially and economically.

The French also made Tunisia's role as a supplier of raw materials and a market for the colonisers' completed goods even stronger by putting in place trade monopolies and tariffs. The coloniser's economic despotism harmed Tunisia's local enterprises and crafts, which made it harder for Tunisians to remain financially independent. It wasn't true that modern facilities like trains and ports were designed to make trade simpler; they were built to make it easier to get Tunisian resources out of the nation to sell. These acts rendered the country even more of a subordinate in the imperial system. Tunisia's economy became dependent on unfair and exploitative employment, with low pay and bad working conditions. Colonial economic oppression created the unjust and unequal institutions that Tunisia still has to struggle with today. The aftermath of Tunisia's economic turbulence continues to impede the achievement of economic justice, advancement, and prosperity.

Cultural Exchanges and Resistance Movements

During the colonial period, cultural connections between

Tunisia and France broke the rule of unequal power dynamics. During the colonial period, there were changes in society and the spread of systems and customs.

When the two civilisations came together, their different ways of life, beliefs, and customs mixed. At the same time, it pushed people to fight back and make a good statement about being Tunisian. All of these elements helped shape the Tunisian social fabric, conscience, and the determination to fight back. French colonial and indigenous Tunisian cultures facilitated hybridisation, resulting in the convergence of numerous aspects from both populations to create a comprehensive Tunisian-French nexus. Colonialism had the biggest effects on the law, language, education, and city planning. The blending of French and Tunisian cultures, including the French language, rituals, and customs with indigenous Tunisian traditions, created a complex social and cultural landscape that reflected a duality in the world. The connected culture also caused problems and fights. This caused the end of proxy rule in Tunisia. The colonisers, who were largely French overlords in Tunisia, had many problems with native artists, intellectuals, and the authority of religion. People employed written, drawn, and spoken words, especially in religious groups, to fight against and safeguard the declining culture of Tunisia. The mixing of cultures makes a thick curtain that covers the numerous levels of cultural identity.

Colonial interactions changed the Tunisian identity, which made people question who they were in response to colonial powers. People changed who they were by taking on new customs, claiming their independence, and feeling a lot of pride in their country. During this time, Tunisian identity developed as a blend of several traditions; Tunisian culture was uniquely Tunisian. Tunisian culture also highlighted how vital it was for people to be proud of their culture and defend it, as well as how brave their forefathers were to do so. Tunisian culture was very much and positively Tunisian. The one-way influences showed that trade works, but having more than one influence can make communication more valuable and useful.

The Impact of Social Stratification in the Region

The colonial relationship between Tunisia and France had a huge effect on the way people in Tunisia's culture thought about socioeconomic class. After the French protectorate was set up, there were two systems: the French added their own hierarchy and structure to the existing Tunisian social order. This layer made the social structure even more convoluted by modifying how power worked and how different social classes could access and control resources.

When colonisation first started, the upper class of landowners, clients, merchants, and religious leaders had to deal with a new group of people: the French settlers. These folks had just become leaders in the military and government and oversaw the economy and politics. The French-backed legal system made things worse for the colonial underclass by giving people from different social classes unequal access to land, business, and legal rights. The colonial powers devised a set of regulations that helped certain groups and hurt others, which made matters even worse. The French government was quite strict and nasty. It punished and limited people who were termed "resistors" and "opponents", while helping and rewarding those who worked with them. These strong consequences for the social class system made the difference between the rich and poor even wider. They also imposed a burden on the lower class's resources and made Tunisian society more grievance-driven.

The fact that jobs and schools were not evenly spread out also revealed that society was separated into classes.

The French's selective education programmes were aimed at making the colonial government loyal. These rules made it such that only rich people and their friends in different social circles could get "elite" jobs and go to "elite" schools. This made it considerably less likely that most Tunisians would be able to improve their social standing. To understand the heart of the colonial centre and the economic activities that happen in the urbanised social division regions, you need to know how Tunisians live. Colonialism developed new economic systems and ways to generate money that were very advantageous to the capitalists who were involved. On the other hand, the rise in social standing and commercial chances made life difficult for farmers, workers, and traditional artisans. Colonialism changed the way power, the economy, and chances operated in Tunisia a lot, which changed the social order a lot. When Tunisia became independent, it was clear why the people wanted to be free. Before and after colonialism, Tunisia's structure was considerably different.

The Mind and Politics Awakening

Tunisia's political and social landscape changed in a big

way throughout the late 1800s and early 1900s, changing the country's path forever.

This epoch offered new ideas and mingled social, cultural, and political elements, which made Tunisia's national identity stronger and made people wish to be free more. Intellectuals, writers, and activists were very against the colonial denial of freedom and independence. A big element of this process was bringing back Tunisia's culture and eliminating colonial efforts to erase native identity. Intellectuals and thinkers have deep conversations on Tunisia's history, culture, and even language. This revival of culture and pride must have brought back a new surge of national identity and solidarity. At the same time, the social and political structure of society began to evolve into a more modern form. The rise of new political parties and groups in the area helped the people move forward and fight back against colonial control in Tunisia. There were a lot of various political ideas, opinions, and structures in movements like this, ranging from small adjustments to big, revolutionary ones that would affect Tunisia's destiny. The passion and energy of these ideas made many people in society angry and brought them together in the name of freedom and independence.

Political and intellectual elites also took it upon themselves to spearhead the transition by persuading the people to support them and asking for a free and independent Tunisia. These leaders' speeches, publications, and activities drew Tunisians together and made them more conscious of the challenges they were having with money and jobs. Tunisia's political and intellectual activities were part of a worldwide movement to end colonialism and give people the right to choose their own future. Tunisia wanted to express its support for those countries that were colonised and seek support for its battle against colonialism in return. Tunisia's fight for freedom has been stronger throughout this moment of action, and it has been presented in the correct global context. The time of political and intellectual activity helped the nationalist movement in Tunisia expand. Tunisia's active phase at this time sparked thinking, action, and determination that helped the country find its place in the world and remember how it affects collective memory. Tunisia has grown the most over this time.

The Rise of Nationalist Ideas

The evolution of nationalist ideology about Tunisia's pursuit of independence was superficial and inadequate.

The mobilisation of larger groups of individuals also helped them understand nationalism better. Nationalist movements, like political movements to promote US nationalism, started from the bottom and worked their way up. Those liked these initiatives to bring together those who had been taken advantage of in numerous ways. As nationalism grew in popularity, nationalist ideology shifted to emphasise economic prosperity, social equality, and the nation's capacity to manage its own resources. The proposed unification framework, which is based on nationalist discourse, was the most essential thing in all political, social, and cultural aspects during the struggle for sovereignty. The political framework for domination demonstrated the sophistication of nationalist thought by refraining from seeking complete control of the country and instead proposing a more advanced system for Tunisia.

In short, the growing advanced and meticulous nationalist attitude in Tunisia is a good means for the country to maintain its independence. The strongly ingrained and resistant spirit of the people came from advanced and systematic nationalist ideas and the country's will to fight for independence.

Key Figures in the National Movement

Tunisia's quest for independence and self-determination was supported by many figures from throughout the world, the region, and the country. Bourguiba became the most prominent figure in the national movement. Bourguiba became a national hero because he was a dedicated and skilled leader for the cause of liberation. The people who battled for independence stood with him and never changed their minds.

Bourguiba was a great visionary in Tunisian history because he was willing to stand up to colonialism. Ben Youssef was a great and strong leader because he could speak well and convince people with his words. He had many people who were very loyal to him. Farhat Hached was very essential in the fight for independence, since he helped build up a number of collaborative projects that highlighted how important it was to have both national and pan-Arab initiatives. His call to action and ideas that brought people together were tremendously significant in the fight against colonialism. Many people were moved by how he saw the future and how he solved problems in a different way.

Along with some of the more well-known leaders, the effort of many lesser-known heroes, such as trade unionists, professors, and activists on the ground, was also vital to keeping the national movement alive. The fight for freedom became increasingly harder because of their dedication, losses, and tireless work towards the objective of an independent Tunisia. The fact that these important people and the public rely on one other indicates how grassroots the national movement was, with many people with various viewpoints and ideas joining for a shared goal. The legacy of these heroes illustrates that the national spirit is still strong in Tunisia today, just like it was when they battled for their freedom and self-rule.

Ways to Become Independent

There were many difficult political, social, intellectual, and international influences that were all intertwined in the years before Tunisia became independent in 1956. The routes to independence were the important events and strategic steps that were taken to help the push achieve self-determination. After World War II, many people in Tunisia wanted to be free.

The nationalist movement, led by important people like Habib Bourguiba and Salah Ben Youssef, got people's attention and leveraged their desire to be free from colonial control. The French government was under more and more pressure, and people all around the world were growing more and more anxious about colonialism. This started a long campaign for freedom. The negotiations and diplomatic efforts that led to independence were full of shrewd adjustments in strategy and power. As the political situation changed, the Tunisian nationalist leaders were able to seek more help from other nations. The civil disobedience and resistance from outside groups also revealed how determined the Tunisian people were to be free and eliminate foreign tyranny. The Tunisian National Pact of 1955 was the first step towards freedom. In an unexpected turn of events, the different organisations in the nationalist movement were able to work together and fight for self-rule. The war of dependence and this sense of solidarity were highly significant for giving Tunisians from diverse classes, cultures, and civilisations a sense of purpose.

Tunisia became totally independent on March 20, 1956, after a long and hard journey. After that, it worked on putting in place and creating a democratic government. Tunisia's independence and the path that led to it still affect the country today. This shows how powerful and determined a nation can be to break free from colonisation.

The Legacy of Colonialism

The French rule of Tunisia from 1881 to 1956 left lasting wounds on the country's economy, politics, and culture that are still visible today. Colonisation had a lasting effect on Tunisia, changing the way people lived, worked, and thought. The changes to Tunisia's social and economic structure during colonialism, such as laws about who can own land and how workers should interact with each other, still have an effect today. Changes in Tunisia's land administration and economy affected how the colonisers ran the country and how the country is run today. Colonisation had a lasting effect on Tunisia's culture and society, which still influences who it is now. Tunisia's art, science, and education still have a lot of French influence. Tunisia's early start in contemporary governance and legal administration systems is what keeps the socio-economic gap from getting worse.

The period of colonisation and its governance and structural control set up a system of central authority and self-government in Tunisia. This had an effect on its independence throughout times of internal turmoil. Also, the structures left behind by colonisation still affect Tunisia's place between continents and how it interacts with the rest of the world. The economics and diplomacy that were developed during colonisation still affect Tunisia's interactions with other countries in the region and around the world. These are, however, the more important repercussions of colonisation, and they depend on how the people of Tunisia view themselves and their national identity. Colonial stories have moulded the country's self-image and understanding of its past. These stories feature themes of struggle and resistance, which are the country's main support. In modern Tunisia, these perceptions can be a source of power. However, some parts of this story may represent a controversial view on national pride, efforts to improve things, social inequality, and the political system. Tunisia's colonial past is quite convoluted and full of inconsistencies. It had a huge effect on the country's independence, and it still does in many ways.

***

⊠References For Further Reading

Foundational & General Histories of Colonial Tunisia

1. Julien, Charles-André. L'Afrique du Nord en marche: Nationalismes musulmans et souveraineté française. 3rd ed., Julliard, 1972.
2. Perkins, Kenneth J. A History of Modern Tunisia. 2nd ed., Cambridge University Press, 2014.
3. Khalidi, Rashid. Sowing Crisis: The Cold War and American Dominance in the Middle East. Beacon Press, 2009. (See Chapter 3: "The Maghrib and the Cold War")

The Protectorate System & Colonial Economy

4. Mabro, Judy, and Robert Ilbert. La Tunisie à l'épreuve du Protectorat: Études d'histoire sociale et économique. Institut de Recherches sur le Maghreb Contemporain, 1995.
5. Poncet, Jean. La Colonisation et l'Agriculture Européenne en Tunisie depuis 1881. Mouton, 1962.
6. Mahjoubi, Ali. L'Établissement du Protectorat Français

en Tunisie. Université de Tunis, 1977.

Social Stratification, Identity, and Cultural Resistance

7. Clancy-Smith, Julia. Mediterraneans: North Africa and Europe in an Age of Migration, c. 1800-1900. University of California Press, 2011.

8. Sebag, Paul. Histoire des Juifs de Tunisie: Des origines à nos jours. L'Harmattan, 1991.

9. Lejri, Lilia. Les Sociétés Arabes au Maghreb et le Changement Social. Cérès Productions, 1985.

10. Abu-Nasr, Jill. "The Tunisian National Movement: A Case Study of a Mobilizing System." The Middle East Journal, vol. 24, no. 4, 1970, pp. 435–452.

The Nationalist Movement & Key Figures

11. Ashford, Douglas E. The Emergence of the Neo-Destour Party in Tunisia: A Case Study of a Maghreb Independence Movement. Princeton University Press, 1965.

12. Bourguiba, Habib. Ma Vie, mes idées, mon combat. Publications du Secrétariat d'État à l'Information, 1977.

13. Kraïem, Mustapha. Nationalisme et Syndicalisme en Tunisie: 1918-1929. Université de Tunis, 1976.

14. Moore, Clement Henry. Tunisia Since Independence: The Dynamics of One-Party Government. University of California Press, 1965.

The Legacy of Colonialism

15. Micaud, Charles A., with Leon Carl Brown and Clement H. Moore. Tunisia: The Politics of Modernization. Praeger, 1964.

16. Hibou, Béatrice. The Force of Obedience: The Political Economy of Repression in Tunisia. Polity Press, 2011.

5
Building National Identity: Education, Memory, and Civic Consciousness

Establishing National Identity After Independence

The post-independence horizon is just as complicated and sensitive to the many strong forces that shape life in a one-nation situation. The political life of a nation is as important as its other parts, since these parts tend to build stories about the state's policies and have a big impact on its history and government. The changes that happen in the social and political systems of political entities after they become independent are important to the main political policies, ideologies, and philosophies that the new state adopts and sees. These elements shape the national identity. Citizenship and the unification of socio-political ideas rely on the management of a substantial populace, social frameworks, and other elements of a nation. Independence, the memory of revolutions, the important contributions of the main nation's history, nationalism, social divisions among groups, and the recognition of state heroes are all important things that help keep social relations, acceptance, and control related to governance structures and political unity. The ideas of citizenship and socio-political factors are linked. In this way, the national sentiment and its celebration also support other things that make the state's cultural identity stronger and encourage people to be included in its formation.

Changes in Education That Shape National Consciousness

Educational improvements for citizens are essential in every country. Tunisia's post-independence educational systems achieved fantastic results in helping its varied citizenry feel like they are part of the country and have a national identity. To promote a sense of patriotism, historical awareness, and civic participation, the Tunisian government made planned changes to the curriculum and the way it was taught. This change in education tried to help the country become independent from colonisation while creating the first cracks in the people's traditional ideology, based on their tribal and regional affiliations.

Education and the new political discourse of Habib Bourguiba founded national feeling and consciousness on the nation-state, thus destroying the remains of tribalism in society—an achievement few Arab states have performed, particularly Libya, Iraq, Syria, Jordan, Saudi Arabia and the Gulf monarchies, etc.

Changes to the curriculum and stories from the past

Educational advancements play a crucial role in shaping the foundation of history while developing the concept of nationality. Schools design their history curriculum to assist those responsible for shaping their country's future. Tunisia's history is not obvious; thus, the changes to the curriculum try to show how national unity has changed since independence. In the last few decades, people who plan and make decisions about education have worked to make the history of the country less nationalistic in school curricula.

Teaching history in old-fashioned terms, like "melanges," is old-fashioned since there are so many different settings and ways to look at things that one might use to completely grasp and describe Tunisia's history and growth. The incorporation of novel viewpoints into Tunisian history facilitates the enhancement of the history curriculum, designed to cultivate an awareness of Tunisia within its historical context and to encourage the development of critical thinking skills.

Pride, belonging, and accountability all come from having a more profound awareness of people and their art and political efforts from the past. Tunisia has a long and fascinating history that is connected to numerous events around the world. This lesson is meant to help the student. More crucially, to appreciate how Tunisia's patriotism, rich history, and civic society have affected fundamental civilisation, or the "advancement of the world," you need to know all three. The combination of these parts satisfies the needs of modern history lectures, which aim to include both original data and modern situations. The major goal is still to show Tunisia's accomplishments in relation to the various, diverse events that have happened around the world, placing them on a timeline of global development.

There is a big worry about how to examine Tunisia's history without losing sight of the bigger picture. The many periods of Tunisia are linked together, which keeps the main features in balance. The primary worry is still about the different sides of Tunisia's history. Looking at the thesis and assumptions of each civilisation or culture could assist in finding holes in analytical studies, synthesis, and political discourse.

History is constantly changing; thus, we need new ideas. To make sure that the curriculum promotes empathy and respect while also allowing for a more inclusive telling of the nation's history, this goal needs to be carefully balanced between celebration and criticism. Tunisia's historical consciousness is constantly changing, so it's important to keep improving the curriculum. Using new and interdisciplinary teaching methods can make the learning environment even better by giving students the skills they need to think critically and actively about the history of their country and picture a future of unity based on shared civic duty and responsibility.

"Memory Politics – Commemorations and National Days"

Memory politics is an important facet in fostering new national identities, curating shared consciousness, and upholding 'cultures'. Commemorations and national days offer citizens opportunities to honour and celebrate historical milestones and values while fostering a sense of belonging. In Tunisia, as with many countries, memory politics helps in coming to terms with the country's struggles and successes. The celebration of Independence Day, Republic Day, and Martyrs' Day are important and integral in this context, as they help Tunisians remember the struggles of the freedom fighters and liberators from colonial subjugation.

These public commemorations are important as they foster national cohesion, and they also help educate the newer generations about history. Interactions with the memory of the past help derive valuable lessons for the current and future shape of the country. The conscious and purposeful act of remembrance ensures that the sacrifices and struggles of the country's people become entrenched in the national identity and consciousness, creating a sense of pride and unity for the country. In addition to this, the celebration of national days helps to underpin and reaffirm the principles and values that the Tunisian state is founded on.

The last stage is the ministry's decade, which is what the last tasks are about. The decade of the ministry can be considered a cabinet that pulls together the surviving treachery, unity, and unification of the logical value structures that exist in the social environment. From a metaphysical perspective, we can perceive the ministry as a fresh manifestation of a dominant and rational global social universe. It makes sense of the existence of social structures and brings individuals together through a shared awareness. In terms of history, the decade of the ministry marks a new stage. The decade can be summed up as the time when a dominant human social environment became more rational and unified. The ministry's ten years bring about a big transformation in how values are connected in the prevailing social milieu and its social institutions. The new social world illustrates how the dominant rationality of local cultures operates within various social contexts, including free systems and unified social systems, such as those found in a unifying world.

Anthems, flags, and symbols help foster a sense of belonging among people.

By combining a sense of ownership and oneness, symbols, flags, and anthems help build a national identity. A flag, for example, is a picture of a country, its values, and its successes. Each flag is a picture of the country's identity and has a lot of meaning that people frequently miss. The colours, emblems, and other parts of the flag also have a lot of meaning. All of this could mean that there is a fierce fight over identity, cultural values, and common beliefs in the country and around the world. It is your job as a citizen to know the flag, its history, and what it represents. To foster a sense of accomplishment and patriotism, songs must be met with equal respect and pride. These songs make the idea of nationality, solidarity, and pride stronger. The goal is to bring together the country's history and principles with the power of its people and culture. It's likely that each of the anthems will bring up strong feelings of patriotism and deeply held values. The whole process of putting together and writing a flag's anthem also brings up strong feelings of patriotism and ideals. Acceptance of national belongings goes hand in hand with civic devotion to the country. This process creates a sense of belonging for everyone while also accepting the diversity that exists in society.

Teaching people about the meaning of these symbols helps them understand and accept each other, which strengthens their loyalty to the country's values and ideals. When people raise the flag, sing the national song, or do something else that is important to the country, they can show their pride in the country and work together for a common goal. In addition, the flag and other national symbols are purposely put in numerous public locations, on official papers, and in works of art to show that they are available to everyone. Therefore, when people use these national symbols, they are also showing that they are united and have a shared goal.

On the other hand, these symbols can also spark discussion and thought. Societal change, shifting viewpoints, and historical revisionism necessitate a reevaluation of the symbols employed for representation and inclusivity. Consequently, prolonged consideration, along with documentation and pragmatic reasoning, is necessary to determine the applicability of the identified symbols, given that the country is not a static entity. In this sense, flags, symbols, and anthems can't be reconciled because the symbols of a nation are constantly changing, even as they bring people together. This kind of arrangement shows how complex and rich a nation's identity is.

Civic Education and Political Socialisation

Civic education is essential for helping people in every culture form political opinions and act in a certain way. It includes both formal and informal ways for people to learn about their rights and duties and how their government works. Civic education has been a key part of Tunisia's nation-building process since it became independent. It aimed to cultivate a culture of active citizenry and the acceptance of democracy among the people. Incorporating civic education into the official school system contributes to cultivating a politically informed and involved population. Students learn about democracy, the rule of law, the preservation of human rights, and what effective governance looks like in the classroom. Students are also taught how to think critically and look at the state of politics and society to have a good awareness of civic concerns and a responsible attitude towards them. In addition, civil society groups, community groups, and governments teach and put into action civic education. These groups give young people the chance to practice leadership, community service, and other civic activities, which helps them understand how important it is to be engaged citizens.

Political socialisation and civic education are processes that influence social ideas, behaviours, and attitudes. Political culture includes people's views, actions, and attitudes. Families, friends, the media, and schools are all places where social learning and transmission happen. Major historical events, revolutionary upheaval, and the processes of decolonisation have influenced the political awareness of the people of Tunisia.

Today, nevertheless, people have new problems and opportunities when it comes to socialising, being politically aware, and doing things. Digital technologies, particularly novel social networks, have profoundly transformed the ways individuals access information, participate in political discourse, and define their self-identity. Consequently, we must conduct a comprehensive analysis of the impacts of these technologies on the political socialisation of adolescents and the broader public.

Civic education and political socialisation are important

for building a nation and keeping democracy going. In this way, giving people the information, ideals, and active abilities they need to participate in civic life helps build a politically and socially integrated country.

Media as a Means of National Conversation and Cohesion

Communication media provide people more ways to express and shape public opinion and discourse. It helps build a unified national identity by giving people a way to express their culture and share common memories.

By supporting Tunisia and pushing for a good development strategy, the media creates a space for national discourse and helps Tunisians accept a new sense of national identity. TV, radio, newspapers, and the internet are the most important media for the country's growth. A country's foundation is its capacity to get its population involved, especially the people of Tunisia. Media is not just a way to share news; it is also a way for people to see their country in a new light and learn from different points of view. A country can create a space where people can come together as "WE" and discuss their problems by using democratic techniques. Furthermore, the media decides what people need to know and what is significant to them. This goal is met by carefully choosing what to put in newscasts and other shows. The country establishes the limits by manipulating the news and controlling the networks. The media helps individuals become more aware of their country by adding more details to the story. However, it also needs other ways, like education, to make these details clearer and easier to understand. It also helps keep and share the group's memory. The media brings people together by showing them the key areas of the country. In plain English, it creates and shares vital historical stories that help people comprehend the deeper ties that exist in the country.

National media organisations also help people become more aware of their civic duties by promoting a positive view of Tunisia's past, present, and future, as well as pride in the country's history. In the context of digitalisation, social media has been a key part of building a sense of national unity.

Online participants and networks make it easier for people to get involved in public life, allowing them to express their cultural values and respond to social problems. The media and others who provide content need to take on corporate social responsibility by speaking up for ethical behaviour and diversity and battling false news to make sure the digital environment is good enough for productive conversations and understanding. Tunisians can reaffirm parts of their national identity and deepen their relationships with the rest of the globe thanks to new media. Tunisia is working to determine the correct balance between new and traditional media. At the same time, it has to focus on the role of cultural, political, and media leaders in encouraging discussion and unity in the country. The media is the key thing that brings Tunisians together, and they are encouraged to take responsibility for actively helping to build the new tale of the country's history.

Young people should become involved in projects that contribute to nation-building.

It's vital for young people to be involved in the fight for social advancement and development. Getting young people involved in politics and society provides them a sense of ownership and strengthens the pillars of national identity. Youth involvement is important since it encompasses many different things, such as volunteering, community service, being an engaged citizen, and even working in business. Engaging in such activities can give young people a voice in shaping the future of the country.

The education system may be the best way to get young people involved in and interested in the decision-making process. Schools and the education system are the main ways to teach people about citizenship and civic duty. Teachers can assist young people in becoming active and responsible citizens by putting in place systems that turn them into leaders, thinkers, and people who care about others. Also, the addition of mentorship and other clubs provides young people a sense of service and social responsibility, as well as helping them reach their full potential.

Also, using current digital technologies and social media might help young people's problems receive more attention and make it easier for them to become involved in significant issues in the country. The youth can be actively involved by participating in online debates, coming up with and leading online initiatives, and coming up with new ideas. Also, young people need to know how to use the internet safely and be digitally literate so they can participate in important activities that help create the nation.

When activism and technology come together, they can come up with fresh ideas and plan big projects to reach shared goals. Encouraging young people in primary and secondary school to think like entrepreneurs can help the economy grow and bring people together. Starting youth-led businesses, innovation hubs, and social enterprises can encourage creativity and critical thinking. These kinds of projects encourage creativity and an entrepreneurial spirit, while also creating a strong culture of initiative and determination. Both government and non-governmental groups improve the entrepreneurial environment by providing resources, advice, and funding, allowing young people to actively participate in the economy and contribute to the country's social well-being. Lastly, engaging young people in nation-building activities is crucial for the country's growth. With the new educational system, young people can learn, use information technology, and come up with new ideas faster and more effectively than ever before. Young people can help the country grow by coming up with new ways to solve problems and by developing a system that directs the country towards growth in a smart way. Some of these projects include community programmes and projects that help people feel like they belong to their community.

Community programs and local identity projects are important because they can help people feel connected to their countries. These projects protect heritage, promote social cohesion, and give local actors the resources they need to build the nation. In Tunisia, community programmes and projects that focus on local identity have been very important for raising national awareness and promoting development that includes everyone.

To make community programmes stronger and help keep alive the traditional arts, crafts, and customs that make up Tunisia's culture. Communities may protect their distinct customs and make the country more culturally diverse by supporting local craftspeople, cultural festivals, and initiatives to protect history. Folks deepen their ties to their roots and take pride in the country's many cultures when they interact with these folks.

Local identity projects also make people feel more connected to their community and encourage them to be more responsible as a group. Community programmes like neighbourhood clean-ups, youth mentoring, and gardening projects try to get the people who benefit from them to feel like they own them and bring people together.

Some local identity projects also try to deal with historical and community memory on a small scale. Communities want to keep their history and contributions alive and celebrate them through oral history initiatives, local museums, and educational programmes. By controlling the stories that the community tells about itself, the community is trying to make the country's collective memory and its own part in it stronger. To make community programming and local identity projects work, you need to work with the government, civil society, and schools in the area. These identified projects can be very successful and reach a larger community if they encourage cooperation and let it improve the results. Also, having a variety of groups of people involved helps people actively accept a shared vision and work together, which is the basis for long-lasting, community-focused growth. In the end, local programs and community identification projects bring people together and make them feel even prouder of their country. They achieve such results by giving people a way to actively interact with other members of the community in the adoption, civic participation, and cultural identity that is unique to the country. Tunisia may bring its many groups closer together and make society stronger and more open.

Successes and Challenges in the Formation of National Identity

The construction of national identity involves intricate processes that necessitate the examination of diverse sociocultural, historical, and political dimensions within a community. Tunisia has been working on and building a strong national identity since it became independent from colonial rule. This is due to its complex history and many cultural influences. Several successes and challenges have marked its journey. One approach to judge how well national identity is forming is to look at how well different social, ethnic, and religious groups are included and represented. Consistent inclusion of minority viewpoints in the prevailing national identity narrative strengthens social cohesiveness and integration. Measures aimed at including everyone in society in the education of citizens about their rights and obligations, as well as civic efforts aimed at fostering a sense of belonging in society, are just as vital.

We need to look at the problems that arise when forming a national identity one at a time. One of the more pressing problems is the need to bring together different historical accounts and the memory wars that have produced division and conflict in society. Engaging in discussions about reinterpreting historical events, cultural symbols, and representations to support national identity while respecting differences is a challenging yet essential conversation that must occur. The difficulties of advancing technology and globalisation through transnational sources add another layer to the process of building a unique national identity through a web of interconnection. The quick expansion of digital forms of mass media, pop culture, and globalised events, which are both valuable and complicated, means that we need to come up with policies and plans that take into account how global and local identities fit together. The complicated and varied structures of political belief systems, as well as the mechanisms of controlling power both inside and outside of a country, have made it harder for national identity to flourish and change naturally. It is challenging to create a uniting national story because you have to do it while keeping in mind the freedom and power that diverse groups in society have. The uniting story hides the need for historical justice and reconciliation, as well as the real structures of unfinished political business.

In short, looking at how national identity was built and what it has done and what it has had to deal with in Tunisia gives a different picture about strength, change, and hope. It stresses the need to build a social identity that is both integrative and inclusive. This means that it should consider the past, the present, the challenges of a changing world, and what it means to be Tunisian. In the end, the procedures and activities that go into building a national identity in Tunisia show how hard people are working to bring together the many different parts of a complicated and changing nation.

***

References For Further Reading

Foundational Theories of Nationalism and Nation-Building

1. Anderson, Benedict. Imagined Communities: Reflections on the Origin and Spread of Nationalism. Revised ed., Verso, 2006.
2. Gellner, Ernest. Nations and Nationalism. 2nd ed., Cornell University Press, 2008.
3. Hobsbawm, Eric, and Terence Ranger, editors. The Invention of Tradition. Cambridge University Press, 1983.

Education and Curriculum as a Nation-Building Tool

4. Brown, L. Carl. "Bourguiba and the Tunisian Nation." The Middle East Journal, vol. 19, no. 3, 1965, pp. 329–343.
5. Barakat, Halim.The Arab World: Society, Culture, and State. University of California Press, 1993.
6. Gardinier, David E. "The Historical Context of Educational Development in Tunisia." The Journal of Modern African Studies, vol. 7, no. 4, 1969, pp. 579–594.

Memory Politics, Commemoration, and Symbolism

7. Olick, Jeffrey K. The Politics of Regret: On Collective Memory and Historical Responsibility. Routledge, 2007.
8. Nora, Pierre. "Between Memory and History: Les Lieux de Mémoire." Representations, no. 26, 1989, pp. 7–24.
9. Elgenius, Gabriella. Symbols of Nations and Nationalism: Celebrating Nationhood. Palgrave Macmillan, 2011.

Civic Education, Media, and Youth Engagement

10. Dewey, John. Democracy and Education: An Introduction to the Philosophy of Education. Macmillan, 1916.
11. Anderson, Jon W. "The Internet and Islam's New Interpreters." New Media in the Muslim World: The Emerging Public Sphere, edited by Dale F. Eickelman and Jon W. Anderson, Indiana University Press, 2003, pp. 45–60.
12. Dhillon, Navtej, and Tarik Yousef, editors. Generation in Waiting: The Unfulfilled Promise of Young People in the Middle East. Brookings Institution Press, 2009.

Tunisia-Specific Case Studies and Legacy

13. Perkins, Kenneth J. A History of Modern Tunisia. 2nd ed., Cambridge University Press, 2014.
14. Willis, Michael J. Politics and Power in the Maghreb: Algeria, Tunisia and Morocco from Independence to the Arab Spring.

6
The Demography of Cohesion: Minorities, Integration, and Political Insignificance

Minorities, Integration, and Political Insignificance

Historical Context of Demographic Composition

The demographic profile of Tunisia is a complicated interaction between its constituent cultural parts. This arose from the activities of many civilisations, from the Phoenicians down to the Romans, Vandals, Byzantines, Arabs, Ottomans, and even Europeans. Tunisia today is a fusion of all these factors, which explains the cultural diversity and plurality of Tunisian society. The social circuit that Tunisia formed with these civilisations serves as the basis for Tunisia's cultural pluralism today. The complex interactions among these civilisations resulted in a unique social-cultural framework that blended various traditions, cultures, and languages.

This social heritage that Tunisia developed from centuries of trade, of which conquest and colonialism formed a significant part, served as a precursor for many other civilisations, such as Berbers, Andalusians, Ottoman Turks, and even Europeans, that settled in the region. This plurality, as well as the demographic profile of Tunisia, is a reflection of the many cultural layers that history has provided to the country, which is a testament to the interconnectedness of the diverse parts that make up Tunisia's very identity. Moreover, the complex trade influences that Tunisia had with these civilisations deepened the cultural intricacies of the region.

A kaleidoscopic and complex demography shaped by different historical events continues to impact the social fabric of contemporary Tunisia.

The Role of Minorities in Shaping National Identity

The presence of minority groups enhances and broadens the national identity of any nation, as they participate in the complex cultural and social mosaic of a country. In Tunisia, the addition of different minority groups throughout the country's history has enriched and augmented the collective identity of the nation. Such minorities, by their narratives, traditions, and languages, have woven their culture with the dominant culture, thus transforming the social fabric of a country. Their efforts have countered the idea of a mono-ethnic national identity, accentuating the pluralistic and intricate nature of Tunisian society. This interaction between the majority and minority groups has led to a shift in the national identity, one that promotes acceptance and diversity. Building a comprehensive and unified national narrative requires acknowledging the distinctive roles and views of minority communities. In addition, minority communities are often the bearers of ideas and experiences, which the nation's historical, political, and social discourse have greatly benefited from.

Contemplating the role of minorities in the formation of Tunisia's identity provides an opportunity for society to advance in the direction of more holistic and representative understandings of its collective narrative. However, it's important to note that minorities' role in building national identity is both vertical and horizontal. While minorities draw from the overarching identity, they are also influenced and shaped by the dominant culture, making the processes of exchange, interaction, and acculturation continuous. Thus, the relationship between the identities of the majority and minorities is not static but rather flexible and in constant change. Recognising and appreciating the different ways in which minorities shaped the Tunisian national identity will augment the social cohesion and resilience of the nation, cultivating an ecosystem in which disparate identities and perspectives are embraced and prominently included in the ongoing construction of Tunisia's narrative.

Strategic Action and Policy Structures

Strategic action and policy structures are vital to achieving peaceful coexistence and prosperity within a pluralistic society. We will scrutinise diverse strategies and policy frameworks that aim to fully integrate minorities into a country's socio-economic ecosystem.

Integration is the active and purposeful effort to ensure people of different backgrounds have a place and contribute to society culturally, economically, and politically. Policy structures play a critical role in the general discourse and practice of the integration of minorities policy, as they set the parameters within which equal treatment, action, and social integration are legally and administratively enforced. A successful integration policy is one that uses a far-reaching approach to deal with the rest of the integration policy—education, employment, health, language, and culture— at the same time. Policies should be developed that not only recognise the varying needs of different minority communities and the structural barriers they face, but also provide the means through which they can access the resources of a wider society. In addition, frameworks need to incorporate the promotion of intercultural dialogue, respect, and culture. Strategic integration plans can promote unity by treating diversity as an advantage, not a division. When evaluating the effectiveness of integration policies, the level of social inclusion, economic participation, and political participation extended to the elites should also be examined. Systemic inequity and socio-economic inequality must be addressed as a primary condition for the full participation of all members of society in resources and opportunities.

Furthermore, the framing and operationalisation of integration plans can greatly benefit from the situational analysis of international 'best practices' and comparative studies. We should use the internal context of the country and the valuable experience of other countries to enhance integration policies. Conversely, the existing policies and legislative frameworks regarding integration will influence the development of new integration policies. The policies on integration will define the area of interaction between all legal, structural, political, and civic integration dimensions. In all sectors, the government should focus on the frameworks that will enable it to integrate society effectively, ensuring that no member feels excluded. Every member of society should be provided the opportunity to participate in their fullest potential to be able to build a society where people appreciate and acknowledge the value of everyone in society.

Educational Outreach and Civic Engagement

Educational outreach and civic engagement facilitate active

participation and encourage a sense of community belonging.

Schools, universities, and community centres serve as foundations for promoting civic responsibility and valuing inclusivity. They can achieve this by introducing multicultural curricula and fostering intercultural relationships. This will instil respect, as well as understanding, among students who come from various cultures. Instruction will not be limited within the four classroom walls but will prepare all students for the global village. The students will understand the importance of civic responsibility and actively participate in various programs. Examples of such programs include volunteers, community-based associations, and youth centres. The programmes increase interaction and collaboration for the common good in the region. They serve as social unifiers and strengthen trust. They also give marginalised communities the opportunity to share their issues and propose solutions aimed at creating a better society.

Policymakers, community leaders, and education stakeholders need to demonstrate their willingness to include civic responsibility and diversity in their agendas. Community leaders should not wait for others to initiate such programmes on their behalf. They need to invest in communication that crosses political, cultural, and educational boundaries. Schools, as the first institutions trained in diversity, should use this offering as a foundation for positive identity recognition. We should encourage active participation in the implementation of democratic and civic social values within society. The leaders should also adopt a democratic method of governance to maintain harmony within all social circles.

Using technology and online resources has the potential to improve outreach activities and public engagement efforts. Resources, such as online learning materials, virtual exchange programs, and community forums, can facilitate people's engagement with different parts of the world. Technology can also help outreach and public engagement activities transcend physical boundaries, allowing connections with people from diverse backgrounds.

To conclude, outreach activities and engagements are critical to instil a sense of belonging and foster intercultural skills and collaboration in a multicultural society. Accepting cultural diversity, empathy, and civic participation are essential to the creation of a society where a person can feel appreciated and respected and contribute as a part of a society to shape the future.

Cultural Pluralism and Social Harmony

Social cohesion and inclusivity in a society need the incorporation of cultural pluralism and social harmony. It is also important to bring in and encourage a bond of unity within and among the people to achieve a greater sense of community. The advancement of cultural pluralism and social harmony is essential in Tunisia, a country with a unique and rich history of cross-cultural exchange and coexistence .

The current section focuses on the various components fostering cultural pluralism alongside social peace, specifically the social instruments that integrate disparate populations into peaceful cohabitation. Cultural pluralism entails the reception of varied cultural identities while remaining within the bounds of an encompassing society. It accepts the existence of various cultural layers while advocating for understanding and reciprocity. It further aims at the retention of customs and traditions that form part of the heritage within the multicultural society. In contrast, social harmony involves the degree to which individuals from various social cultures live and work together for the advancement of society. It involves the development of social empathy, lowering discriminatory barriers, and fostering a social landscape for all, irrespective of their standing. The attainment of cultural pluralism and social harmony is a challenge for both state and non-state actors. For example, encouraging policies on cultural exchange programs, multicultural activities, and cross-cultural contact is vital for promoting understanding and respect among different groups. The investment in cultural facilities like museums and heritage sites is further evidence of the country's commitment to its cultural diversity.

Incorporation of multicultural education into the curriculum and promoting awareness of various traditions, coupled with fostering the values of acceptance and tolerance, can help schools cultivate social and cultural pluralism. Besides, the promotion of socio-economic initiatives addressing the economic plight of marginalised communities can help enhance social cohesion, as there is a strong correlation between economic and social cohesion. Providing financial support for marginalised communities for the purpose of entrepreneurship and vocational training, along with equitable employment opportunities, can help reduce the structural inequities that hinder social cohesion. Moreover, community development initiatives that enhance equitable distribution of healthcare, housing, and other infrastructure can promote social integration, thus resulting in improved welfare for people of all social and cultural diversities. For all these reasons, pursuing cultural pluralism along with social harmony is important to provide a sense of equity and belonging to the people within the society. Tunisia has significant potential to progress from merely celebrating diversity and social cohesion to actively incorporating social pluralism, which is essential for fostering both cultural pluralism and social harmony necessary for prosperity.

Economic Participation and Community Development

Participation in the economy and the development of communities have important and positive impacts on social solidarity and the economic wellbeing of a country. In the case of Tunisia, it is important to the social fabric of the country to let minority groups take part in economic and community development. Initiatives to improve the economic situation of the minorities in Tunisia needed to be multidimensional by including the range of employment, self-employment, skills, and financial services. If Tunisia creates a proper economic climate and an enabling environment to empower the economic growth of minority communities, it can take advantage of the social cohesion dividend that it will provide. Community development programs for minorities should emphasise economic, social, and physical infrastructure while alleviating unique and intersectional disadvantages. The imbalance in the country can be rectified by removing the infrastructural, healthcare and educational, and vocational training deficit in these minority-populated areas that promote equity and a sense of achievement. Enhancing the entrepreneurial environment in these marginalised communities will not only stimulate local economies and job growth but also foster innovation.

By spurring small business initiatives, encouraging the forming of market linkages, and improving access to credit and other financial resources, ownership integration and economic vibrancy can be greatly achieved in the targeted communities. The public sector, private sector, civil society, and all other international actors collaborate to foster the economic development of the minority population. With the help of the relevant expertise, resources, and network, targeted initiatives can be developed to address the economic and social inequalities of the targeted population. The initiatives need to be inclusive to promote economic growth of the community as well.

Community development, economic participation, and, most importantly, the active engagement of economically marginalised groups in the community to address poverty and inequality are crucial. The comprehensive development of investment and economic engagement can replace the social disparity with social cohesion and prosperity accompanied by growth.

Political Representation and Minority Voices.

Political representation is important, especially in a democracy, where there's a need to balance and accommodate all positions and views concerning a decision. It is particularly relevant to minority communities, whose needs and expectations differ more from those of the majority in a democracy.

Tunisia's case is particularly intriguing because of its multicultural nature and the additional problem of the immobility of the political system. For a long time, the minority populations within the country have experienced worrying and debilitating disenfranchisement because of a lack of political representation. These issues have all attempted to respond in some significant way to the problem and, to varying degrees of success, have brought about changes in the legal framework, socio-political actions, and advocacy campaigns. They have been careful to implement democracy at the grassroots level and provide favourable political encouragement for minority populations to undertake public roles. They have also been at the centre of campaigns to reverse minority apathy and political disinterest that have been pervasive in certain community actions. These undertakings have been placed within the wider framework of the establishment of various consultative and advisory bodies designed to hear and respond to the issues of minority populations. Despite the greatest efforts of all parties, the issue of politically effective representation remains unresolved. The slanted and politically isolated aspects, along with economically unequal and stratified societies, class divisions, and entrenched power systems derived from oppressive socio-political structures, all hinder the absorption and political integration of minority populations. In some cases, primary and secondary bias within certain minority populations that are politically stagnant and passive adds to the problems of invisibility in the political system.

The intricacies of intergroup relations alongside identity

politics make it more difficult to provide equitable representation to every group. Meeting these challenges requires a broad approach that includes both systems and attitudes to the political neglect of minorities. It requires primary co-operation and active communication between state bodies, civil society and representatives of minority groups to design appropriate policies and practices that enhance inclusion and equity. In addition, nurturing a political culture infused with equity and respect for differences is important to establishing the setting in which minority populations can flourish and reshape the country's destiny. By remaining committed to collaboration, Tunisia can aim to achieve a more representative participatory democracy that practices equity and pluralism. This will, in turn, strengthen the social cohesion and the sense of belonging of every citizen.

Challenges of Assimilation and Resistance to Change

Diverse societies face significant challenges to their social cohesion whenever assimilation, or resistance to change, occurs. The act of assimilation, in which minorities embrace the dominant culture and the values of mainstream society, comes with a great deal of resistance.

Such resistance can arise from fears and concerns regarding discrimination and cultural loss integrated within historical identities. One counterargument against immigration is that it can lead to the disassociation of cultural identity and cause turmoil. To protect against political pluralism and radicalism, minority communities will engage in cultural practices. Similar to these communities, the fear of losing their predominating significance compels them to resist assimilative pressures. Distrust in change is equally valid regarding the dominant social structures. For a plethora of reasons, including discrimination and intersectional discrimination, minority groups are inclined to view the act of assimilation and its processes as something dangerous to self-governing autonomy. The neglect exhibited by national-level feminist institutions worsens both the problem and the resistance to assimilation. The vicious neglect regarding movement assimilation includes, alongside social discrimination, paradoxical structures of economic opportunity. Dismal socioeconomics views this process in opportunistic terms and frames it within assimilation. The decision to resist or embrace assimilation inextricably links to the struggle between social segregation and economic division. The various sets of values and principles represent significant barriers to the process. The process of assimilation is complicated for the entire country.

Incorporating religious, ethical, and moral differences could make the process of assimilation more difficult. We must strategically approach resistance to change and the challenges that assimilation poses. This includes the formulation of protective and inclusive atmosphere policies that permit loyalty to the different mosaic elements of the society and, simultaneously, to the mosaic that emerges. Additionally, overcoming biases, fostering dialogue, building trust, and addressing systemic inequity are essential for facilitating integration and overcoming resistance to the economy of integration. Understanding the assimilation process and the obstacles to its deep structural change requires a balanced and sophisticated comprehension of the entire system. By recognising and resolving these issues, the aim would be to frame a society that alleviates the tension resulting from the process of change and offers the freedom to be different, to be empowered fully, and to embrace cultural identities.

Case Studies of Effective Integration Models

When studying the underlying factors that shape how different nations function, it is important to identify successful integration models that contribute to social harmony and cohesion. This research section analyses case studies from around the world and successful methods of integrating minority populations.

The case study of Canada and its multiculturalism policies is particularly noteworthy. The country has been able to integrate many immigrant communities through government-sponsored language training and cultural awareness programmes, even as they continue to practise their distinctive cultures. Another remarkable case is that of Norway. Norway has extended inclusive education policies to minority groups and has also dedicated healthcare resources to their integration. Through the provision of intercultural services and the encouragement of intercultural contact, Norway has achieved a positive posture in the management of diversity. In addition, the city of Malmö in Sweden has integrated social cohesion and the diversification of urban planning in community development to facilitate social inclusion. This programme focuses on the distribution of public amenities and social services.

In addition, there is the success of integration policies in

Singapore, where proactive housing along with ethnic-inclusive economic policies have aided in the peaceful melting of various ethnic groups. These case studies which demonstrate the success of integration are particularly important for their emphasis on inclusiveness, equity, and cultural appreciation. In looking at these success stories, Tunisian policymakers and practitioners of social integration will uncover important lessons in fostering social cohesion and inclusiveness in their mosaic society.

Prospects for Future Cohesion in a Diverse Society

In a diverse society, cohesion is dependent on the interplay of changes in population structure, physical and cultural sociopolitical changes, and systems of values. These structural elements border a society in Tunis that is rich in ethnic, religious, and linguistic diversity. For these elements to produce societal cohesion, pluralism along with a common national identity needs to be strongly developed. With the evolution of Tunisian society in the context of the rest of the globe, the ability to cultivate the factors supporting the coherence and peaceful social integration of its constituents deserves attention.

An area of concern that can extend or limit the prospects of societal cohesion is the inclusion of people in the policies and activities aimed at promoting social integration and equity in representation. Tunisia, through constructive cultural policies that address cultural grievances and promote minority participation in decision-making, can start building a better integrated and inclusive society. In addition, creating a sense of belonging to a nation, beyond personal identities, can serve to unify people and strengthen the idea of belonging to a diverse Tunisia with common heritage and common bonds. A major area of influence in the future of societal cohesion is education. By integrating diversity and inclusion as a foundation in educational curricula and thereby highlighting the achievements of all sectors of society, Tunisia can produce a future citizenry that appreciates diversity and is willing to promote inclusion. Outreach education programmes that foster intercultural understanding and tolerance, as well as responsible citizenship, can enhance social cohesion through the integration of divergent social clusters. In addition, the future prospects of societal cohesion require the attainment of equity and inclusive growth.

Tunisia can promote equal access to social opportunity by fostering equity in access to opportunity, resources, and services across communities so that every individual contributes to the development of the nation and feels valued and empowered. By promoting entrepreneurship, skills, and employment opportunities tailored to various demographics, we can strengthen social cohesion through the generation of economic agency. The evolution of Tunisia's political landscape also impacts the trajectory of social cohesion. The absence of trust and confidence in democracy can be addressed by ensuring that minority governance voices are empowered, alongside fostering open dialogue and participatory decision-making. Efforts to reduce discrimination and marginalisation while also respecting the rights of all citizens, regardless of their origin, strengthen the foundation for resilient social cohesion and secure borders.

Tunisia's future social cohesion prospects will depend on the integration of diversity issues and the issuance of dominant and divisive social policies. Unity in diversity should be the common value and the fundamental aspect of national identity. Meaningful engagement and contribution from all segments of society to help foster social cohesion is also vital.

Tunisia's celebration of its diversity, alongside its enduring commitment to equity, inclusion, and social justice, will enable it to build a society where differences are no longer just accepted but are embraced as a source of cohesion and advancement.

For Further Reading

General Overview & Historical Context

1. Abu-n-Nasr, J. M. (1987). A History of the Maghrib in the Islamic Period*. Cambridge University Press.
2. Perkins, K. (2014). A History of Modern Tunisia (2nd ed.). Cambridge University Press.
3. Davis, D. (2011). Resurrecting the Granary of Rome: Environmental History and French Colonial Expansion in North Africa. Ohio University Press.

Minorities, National Identity, and Cultural Pluralism

4. Maddy-Weitzman, B. (2011). The Berber Identity Movement and the Challenge to North African States. University of Texas Press.
5. Braham, R. (Ed.). (2015). The Vatican and the Holocaust: The Catholic Church and the Jews*. Routledge. (See also: "The Jews of North Africa and the Holocaust").
6. Kymlicka, W. (1995). Multicultural Citizenship: A Liberal Theory of Minority Rights*. Oxford University Press.
7. Parekh, B. (2000). Rethinking Multiculturalism: Cultural Diversity and Political Theory. Harvard University Press.

Strategic Policy, Integration, and Political Representation

8. Bloemraad, I. (2006). Becoming a Citizen: Incorporating Immigrants and Refugees in the United States and Canada. University of California Press.
9. Phillips, A. (1995). The Politics of Presence. Oxford University Press.
10. Organisation for Economic Co-operation and Development (OECD). (2018). Working Together for Local Integration of Migrants and Refugees. OECD Publishing.

Education, Civic Engagement, and Economic Participation

11. Banks, J. A. (Ed.). (2009). The Routledge International Companion to Multicultural Education. Routledge.
12. Putnam, R. D. (2000). Bowling Alone: The Collapse and Revival of American Community. Simon & Schuster.
13. Sen, A. (1999). Development as Freedom. Alfred A. Knopf.

Case Studies of Effective Integration Models

14. Banting, K., & Kymlicka, W. (Eds.). (2017). The Strains of Commitment: The Political Sources of Solidarity in Diverse Societies. Oxford University Press.
15. Vertovec, S., & Wessendorf, S. (Eds.). (2010). The Multiculturalism Backlash: European Discourses, Policies and Practices. Routledge.

Tunisia-Specific Contemporary Analysis

16. Allani, A. (2013). The Post-Revolution Tunisian Constituent Assembly: The Miracle and the Mirage. The Journal of North African Studies, 18(2), 327-335.
17. Gana, N. (Ed.). (2013). The Making of the Tunisian Revolution: Contexts, Architects, Prospects. Edinburgh University

Press.

18. Meddeb, H. (2017). Peripheral Visions: Public, Power, and Performance in the Tunisian Revolution. Columbia University Press.

7
Migration and State Capacity
Managing Contemporary Flows

A Look at the Migration Trends in Tunisia

Tunisia has long been a place where people from all over the world come to live and work. This is because it is located where the Mediterranean Sea meets the rest of Africa. Economic pursuits, political instability in neighbouring nations, and conflicts across the ocean have influenced the continual influx of migrants in Tunisia. Intraregional and international issues dominate the social, economic, and political frameworks that form Tunisia today. It would be an understatement to suggest the movement of population has been unidirectional, especially in the context of Tunisia, which has received migratory inflows from sub-Saharan African nations like Mali, Nigeria, and Ivory Coast. Additionally, wars and other social and political problems trigger migration from the Middle East and North Africa. Sophisticated records of migrant admissions indicate that the number of people entering the country fluctuates with changes in the region and the global economy. We have also witnessed gradual shifts in the patterns of international migration to Tunisia. These trends have led Tunisian authorities and other key decision-makers to devise migration policies that respond to the social effects of migration on Tunisia.

Stakeholders evaluate the intricacies of migration trends, identify obstacles and gaps in demands, and appreciate the value that migrants provide to Tunisia's socioeconomic landscape. This understanding is vital and forms the basis of a sophisticated approach to creating policies that balance the problems of migration with the need for broader societal engagement of migrants.

The historical context of migration and its impact on state capacity

Tunisia's history of migration goes along with the country's growth as a meeting place for many cultures. We can trace this back to ancient times, when the Phoenicians and then the Romans transformed the area. The country's rich history as a focus of cultural, economic, and strategic contacts involves migration. The new food, dialects, and customs that the country enjoyed from the 7th century and the intervening centuries as a result of the conquests and the Ottoman conquest, in addition to colonial extensions, were also of enormous significance. These migrations, alongside the rich Tunisian culture, provided a new religious and ethnic dimension to the region, moulding its character and present society. The socio-political and economic systems emerging from the emigrations are what shaped the state's emigration potential.

From a political standpoint, the management of immigration and the rights of minorities have always been issues for governance. This involves a delicate balancing of national integrity and the availability of cultural space. Socially, migration has been a factor in enhancing the cultural mosaic of Tunisia and the formation of a diversified society. There is a need to acknowledge the fact that the integration of people, social cohesion, and the distribution of services have required substantial planning and modifications from the government. Economically, migration has boosted the diversification of resources, skills, and knowledge brought to the country. Development has been unequal, and competition for resources and facilities has made it hard for governments and diplomats to do their jobs. Understanding the migratory histories existent in many states is vital for seeing alternative possibilities, and Tunisia plays a particularly major role in global migration, which is more integrated and marked by global patterns.

Policy Framework for Migration Management

The socio-political environment of Tunisia, which includes migration, underlines the need to design optimal policies for effective migration handling. Migration, which comprises numerous factors such as the economic, the social, the security, and the humanitarian, requires a strategy that aims to address these various parts. While the policy framework should encourage migration, preserve security, and safeguard fundamental rights and freedoms, it should integrate migrants productively into society to stimulate economic growth and strengthen the cultural mosaic of the country.

Migrant policy should establish processes for the defined enforcement, control, and removal of borders, which include access to and areas of subsequent residence along with their exit. Migrants include individuals whose employment can maintain economic growth, as well as spouses, family members seeking reunification, asylum seekers, and irregular migrants. There should be established and clear policy procedures and rules regarding migrants, as well as the record keeping, rights protection, and abuse or exploitation procedures.

It is important to establish status policies that set the right balance between Tunisia's responsibilities to the world and its own policies. There should be tactics that specify border control, trafficking, smuggling, and migration in response to improved policy.

In such a circumstance, the framework must consider having an international and regional focus while retaining the autonomy of internal approaches. Most importantly, the policy framework has to consider the development of institutional migration management policies and migration policies, as well as the development of related policies. The immigration system, police, and social services require appropriate resources, training, and coordination. Additionally, the framework entails formulating the migration management policy and providing resources and support to promote civil society, academics, and their integration into the migration system. Another key feature of the policy is the development of interagency communications and coordination on the national, subregional, and local territorial levels of the state. This structure enhances the policy by offering a new level of knowledge, data, and a unified governance and decision-making framework to handle migration policy more effectively. Finally, the policy framework needs to include options for migration policy and the ability to adapt to changes in migration, global politics, and social politics. The framework achieves balance and flexibility in reaction to changes in the flow of people by incorporating a formation system, a change system, and intervals that adjust to shifts in migration patterns and national-level responses.

In conclusion, building a complete policy for migration management should be inventive and holistic, focusing on security but also integrating humanitarian issues, promoting integration, and balancing the positive sides of migration.

Tunisia needs a policy framework like this to handle current migration flows correctly and participate in the larger discussion on how to govern migration.

Institutional Roles in Migration Handling

Managing migration is a difficult subject that involves the coordination of numerous organisations within the structure of the Tunisian state. The initial point of contact with emigrants in Tunisia is the Ministry of Interior and the Ministry of Foreign Affairs, who are important to the establishment and execution of emigration policy. Border control, general surveillance, and the implementation of immigration restrictions are the responsibility of the Ministry of Interior, whereas the Ministry of Foreign Affairs participates in international collaboration on migration policy. Together, these organisations are responsible for ensuring national security and border control in Tunisia, while strengthening international connections with key nations during migration. The Ministry of Justice also plays a crucial role in migration through the governance of asylum and the protection of the human rights of migrants and refugees in Tunisia.

In addition to this, the social welfare department works with national and foreign partners to provide social assistance and services to migrants and supports them with their social integration and well-being within Tunisian society. The National Institute of Statistics is an essential contributor to the collecting and analysis of data on migration, as well as the formulation of migration policies and governing structures. Furthermore, the local government's cooperation is vital to the reception and integration of migrants within the area. These institutional duties, in their entirety, embody the integrated approach to managing migration in Tunisia, signalling the government's determination to solve the issues created by the migratory processes. Nevertheless, difficulties like the paucity of funding, the degree of coordination and collaboration among numerous stakeholders, and even the general attitude to migration are all factors that determine the degree to which the institution's duties are effective in handling migration. To solve these problems, government agencies, civic society, and even global players need to work together and stay involved to create complete and integrated systems for managing migration. With the rethinking of institutional roles and strengthening of coordination, Tunisia would immediately boost its ability to respond to the dynamics of migration and, at the same time, support the protection of migrants and the goals of the state.

Socio-economic Implications of Migratory Trends

The migratory phenomenon presents both complexities and opportunities for the host country. When it comes to socio-economic, migration patterns have long-lasting effects on many parts of Tunisian society and the economy. First, migration drives changes in the population and the labour market. The surge in migration adds variety to the labour force and fills difficult-to-staff roles in the under- and over-supplied labour sectors, which can enhance productivity and drive economic growth. It is conceivable and simpler for the economy to grow if the country's construction, agriculture, and service industries are streamlined properly. But the economy would require robust construction policies to support moral workplace settings and positive employee interactions. In addition, migrants contribute to cultural diversification and can encourage cultural exchange. Such action augments the social fabric of the country in addition to improving opportunities for business and creative collaborations. At the same time, however, this cultural diversity can offer social obstacles and tensions regarding self, integration, social harmony, and inclusion, which requires the presence of actual policies and active social cohesion. On the other hand, the social, health, education, and housing services provided to migrants and their families can be significantly enhanced to strengthen public services and infrastructure. The health and active involvement of migrants and their families in the socio-economic system is ensured by their fluent and simple access to the offered services and public infrastructure, which enhances the need for the public to be inclusive and accessible to all.

These factors underscore the necessity of formulating policies that emphasise access, equity, and inclusion in service delivery. Furthermore, the money that Tunisians living abroad send home is a valuable resource for the economy because it helps with foreign currency, investment, and even lowering poverty. Consequently, the maintenance of productive diplomatic relations with the diaspora and the establishment of policies allowing remittances to be used for sustainable development are crucial pillars in Tunisia's projection. The complexity of Tunisia's migratory pattern is visible. It is interwoven with the economy, society, labour force, and culture. These aspects are often labelled as socioeconomic factors. Tunisia is shouldering significant responsibility as a result of complicated socio-economic migratory tendencies. People commonly talk about these as the social and economic effects of moving. To address the problems that arise with migration, we need to use democratic and international methods. The shifting policies should be in line with socio-economic objectives while closing the gaps and the problems that come along with them.

Security Concerns and Migration Control Measures

Migration is one of the things that affects global security, and it has to do with Tunisia. Numerous security risks arise from the influx of migrants, necessitating the establishment of suitable laws and migration control measures. A significant security issue, in this context, is the illegal immigration stream and the criminal activities that come with it, such as human and drug trafficking and terrorism. These activities take advantage of inadequate migration controls and border security and, in this way, represent security dangers both in and out of Tunisia. Therefore, stricter migration controls need to be in place to combat these kinds of dangers. Tunisia has implemented various migration control measures to address security concerns. These are things like better border control, more surveillance, the use of detection and monitoring technologies, and coordination among law enforcement agencies. Also, creating and enforcing immigration control rules and procedures has been very advantageous in stopping illegal immigration and the crimes that come with breaking the law. In addition, cross-border cooperation has greatly strengthened Tunisia's ability to restrict migration by allowing them to share information, work together on operations, and verify that their policies and rules are in line.

Beyond these concerns goes the question of responsible and ethical migration control.

The border control context necessitates the awareness and protection of vulnerable migrants' human rights. It is challenging to design and carry out a policy that deals with both security and humanitarian challenges at the same time. By pushing for the compassionate treatment of migrants, facilitating access to justice, and, if practicable, aiding assimilation, Tunisia's strategy seeks balance. It is important to remember that effective migration control measures should not violate basic human rights or make the migrant community more vulnerable. The ability to integrate security and humanitarian outcomes is a critical factor for establishing migratory governance that is legally respectable and humane. Tunisia's stance in the framework of the conversation is to address security challenges in a principled manner regarding the management of migration.

International Cooperation and Bilateral Agreements

Within Tunisia, international ties and bilateral agreements have a remarkable impact on the management of the present migratory flows. As part of diplomacy, such agreements help facilitate technical bilateral contacts with purposeful collaboration on migration concerns. Within such bilateral agreements, the legal rights and obligations of the migrating and conversing countries are stated, and legal migration procedures, repatriation of migrants, and collaboration on migration problems constitute a dialogue.

These agreements frequently aid in border control, visa facilitation, labour mobility, and safeguarding the rights of migrant workers. Migrants are handled with respect and are kept in order. Migrants in Tunisia benefit from proper agreements that ensure regulated migration and the preservation of their rights. Border control, visa management, and getting rid of migrants are all working. Transnational goals address irregular migration, human trafficking, and transnational crime throughout Tunisia and its target nations. A balanced framework sets these goals, giving equal weight to border security and human rights. These aims balance border security with respect for human rights. International goals include border control and transnational standards. Tunisia's humanitarian migration policies apply to all individuals, regardless of their immigration status. The major participants in these accords are EU countries. Tunisia shares borders with EU member states, and these states are responsible for critical borders that restrict the movement of migrants from Europe to North Africa. Both Europe and North Africa strictly monitor the borders between Tunisia and the EU. The basic borders and border control are based on the borders of Europe, especially the controlled borders of Tunisia. These migration flows have made it challenging for people to get to EU border strategies because the borders are so busy. These agreements also encompass border control, management, and partnership with Maghreb countries to cope with espionage attitudes in Algeria and Libya. Tunisia additionally increases the control of border agreements at its crossing points through processing, collaborative mechanisms, mutual border operations, and support. Border control involves key and cross relations, transnational coordination, and a borderless strategy.

Furthermore, international collaboration and bilateral connections extend beyond security concerns and border control. They also involve issues linked to development, integration, and campaigning for the rights of migrants. Tunisia employs such collaborations to promote the socio-economic integration of migrants, intercultural interactions, and anti-discrimination. Tunisia handles the problems that arise with migration in a way that protects the basic rights and well-being of everyone involved while also getting long-term, comprehensive, and sustainable results. Tunisia needs to keep working with other countries and making agreements with them to build and keep good connections as migration changes. With knowledge of common interests, Tunisia can increase its ability to meet problems and exploit the opportunities of current migrant movements. It can also play a bigger part in the world community by being an active member of the migration policy.

Human Rights Considerations and Migrant Integration

When talking about migration, it's crucial to stress the importance of human rights and the need to help migrants fit in. It is essential to establish a human rights framework that protects the dignity of all individuals, including migrants, whether they have papers or not.

They also have the right to not be treated unfairly and to receive health care, education, and fair treatment at work. Facilitating the social integration of migrants into the host country benefits both the migrants and the host country by promoting social cohesion and overall growth. Migrant integration strategies and activities should be to some extent inclusive of the host nation's citizenship. Beyond the economics of integration, civic and cultural participation are also vital to establishing more integrated societies. Intercultural communication and language training, structural vocational training, and other forms of education address and undertake the issues of migration in the host country. Providing migrants with the required framework and social tools helps them to be full and active participants in the social and economic growth of the host country, which finally contributes to the establishment of a cohesive and inclusive society. It is vital to remember that not all migrants have the same social and economic conditions. Women, children, and refugees are specific and vulnerable populations that face unique difficulties that need more attention. More inclusive gender policies and support structures, as well as legislative mechanisms to cover the gaps in the particular scenarios these women, children, and refugees face, are highly vital. Additionally, the unique circumstances of refugees requiring international protection and the asylum procedures must be acknowledged and respected, as these represent fundamental human rights that should be treated accordingly. Among the various facets of migration that the Tunisian government needs to address, it is vital that the policies created align with human rights standards in the region. Other stakeholders who are gauging the migration policies have the responsibility to comply.

The legislation demands the design and execution of developed programmes that defend the migrants' rights and promote their full integration within the Tunisian social fabric. These kinds of programs meet moral standards and also make room for people to come together and make the country great. It is also the promotion of migrants' integration, alongside the respect and implementation of their rights, which displays a more modern and intelligent approach to dealing with current migratory patterns. Tunisia is able to exhibit an inclusive approach, development of social cohesiveness, and growth of legal protection, which in turn portrays Tunisia as a leader and exemplar of compassion in migrant governance at the international level.

Problems with effective migration governance

The governance of migration presents several challenges for effectively managing the flow of migrants into Tunisia. A primary issue is the lack of accurate statistics and information regarding the migrant community, its demographic characteristics, and its integration into the Tunisian socio-economic framework. Policymakers and important actors in the realm of migration policy development are unable to design well-targeted and evidence-based measures in the absence of reliable and timely data. Furthermore, the current jurisprudence and migration policy may, at times, exhibit deficiencies and internal contradictions, resulting in ambiguity concerning the rights and obligations of migrants and the members of the host society.

Additionally, the enforcement of policies and regulations regarding migration is, in large part, challenging, especially in the distant border areas where the migration control system is, by definition, tenuous. Socio-economic aspects of migration, such as employment and population access to primary services, especially health and education, tend to overextend public facilities and services, which, in turn, gives rise to social unrest. Furthermore, the absence of efficient means of connection and integration between migrants and residents of the receiving societies is frequently articulated via unarticulated social gaps and the presence of linguistic and other hurdles. Security is one of the significant societal gaps. Sophisticated and complicated security concerns have led to the criminalisation of increasingly obscure and globalised cross-border criminal organisations. Most of the security challenges are easier to address than these complicated and cross-border illicit businesses.

To keep up with the changing patterns and routes of migration, border policy and immigration control need to be both strict and flexible. To keep migrants from being exploited and trafficked, law enforcement and oversight need to be cautious. The complexity of international migration involves coordination and cooperation with peers and supranational institutions, often presenting diplomatic and geopolitical challenges. In bilateral and multilateral partnerships, ongoing involvement, coupled with mutual understanding and trust, is essential to address common migration challenges and ensure the orderly transit of individuals across borders. In Tunisian social contexts, unresolved concerns may arise from social resistance and xenophobia directed at the border community. The governance concerns generated by the complications of migration can be summed up by the expression, "However deep the roots of prejudice are, inclusiveness and diversity can be nurtured." We must take action because we understand the difficulty involved. This in particular is why migratory governance in deep adaptation is, in the instance of Tunisia, best tackled in terms of maximum disentangled engagement to responsiveness that is indicated to the opacity and fragmentation existing in the agency. This is true for Tunisia.

Future Directions and Policy Recommendations

In Tunisia, the only way forward for migration governance is to adopt a policy approach that addresses the key challenges underlying its geopolitical and organisational difficulties. While the nation seeks to handle the complications around its borders, it will need a proactive migration policy that balances global norms with local realities. Knowing where people move is still a key part of making policy. Policy action to improve the contributions of migrants and limit the negative repercussions of migration on the host communities, together with regionally specific policy action, is vital. Then, creating effective policies would require complex coordination both within the country and with other countries. It is important to have enough cross-border collaborations. Finally, the integration of institutions further improves migration governance by strengthening coordination. Better control of borders at the municipal and regional levels, easier asylum processes, and steps to include migrants all help the state control and manage migration better. Better cooperation between agencies makes internal governance and border control for migration better by making it easier for law enforcement, border control, migration, and refugee aid services to work together. In addition, Tunisia should increase migration policy cooperation and bilateral treaties to effectively regulate migrations within the country.

Engaging with neighbouring countries, regional organisations, and international groups can facilitate the establishment of common rules for migration, assistance, and information sharing. Tunisia may address migration as a geopolitically significant global issue by engaging in multilateral forums and international agreements, thereby leveraging worldwide best practices through global collaboration. In light of these inspections, adopting a migration policy and procedures that are based on human rights is a requirement. A rights-based migration strategy which respects and defends the rights of migrants, supports non-discrimination, and encourages social inclusion is vital. Affirming the dignity and agency of migrants in all categories, including irregular ones, is, at the very least, a fulfilment of Tunisia's international duties and socially desirable for the objectives of national integration and harmony. In this context, Tunisia exemplifies migratory governance; it is crucial to have proactive policies with enough resources for ongoing monitoring, evaluation, and required revisions. Migratory movements as a policy focus are a continually changing and dynamically altering group of occurrences. It is crucial to be proactive so that as movement occurs on the ground, corresponding policy instructions and measures are in place. Innovation is vital, but it's equally important to make evidence-based decisions about procedures and include everyone so that migration policies are relevant, implemented, and effective.

Tunisia will become a leader in progressive and sustainable government on migration issues and changes by following these strategic directions and suggestions.

***

References For Further Reading

The Constitutional Revolution and Identity Politics

1. Marks, M. (2014). Convince, Coerce, or Compromise? Ennahda's Approach to Tunisia's Constitution. Brookings Institution.
2. Wolf, A. (2019). Tunisia's Compromise Constitution: A Model for the Region? The Journal of North African Studies, 24(1), 1-23.
3. Gana, N. (2013). The Making of the Tunisian Revolution: Contexts, Architects, Prospects. Edinburgh University Press.

Salafism and Religious Polarisation

4. McCarthy, R. (2015). Salafism and the State: Islamic Activism and National Identity in Contemporary Tunisia. Bloomsbury Academic.
5. Merone, F. (2015). Enduring Class Struggle in Tunisia: The Fight for Identity beyond Political Islam. Mediterranean Politics, 20(2), 1-18.

Transitional Justice and Collective Memory

6. Fisher, J. (2019). Tunesien: Das Versprechen der Transitional Justice. Eine Analyse der Konfliktbearbeitung nach dem Arabischen Frühling. Springer VS.

7. Slyomovics, S. (2021). The Tunisian Truth and Dignity Commission and the Politics of Victimhood. The Journal of North African Studies, 26(5), 881-900.

Civil Society and Counter-Movements

8. Beaumont, P. (2013). Tunisia's Seculturalists: The Fight for a Civil State. The Guardian. (And subsequent academic analyses of the "Tunisian League for the Defense of Secularism").
9. Allal, A., & Geisser, V. (2018). Tunisie: Une démocratisation au-dessus de tout soupçon? Critique Internationale, 81(4), 21-42.

The Crisis of the Democratic Model

10. Ayari, M. B. (2021). Tunisia: The Revolution as a Cartography of Power. The Carnegie Endowment for International Peace.

11. Boubekeur, A. (2017). Islamists, Secularists and Old Regime Elites in Tunisia: Bargained Competition. Middle East Policy, 24(3), 55-71.

12. International Crisis Group. (2021). Addressing the Crisis of Confidence in Tunisia. Middle East and North Africa Report No. 221.

8
Ideological Divisions Within National Unity
Islamists, Secularists, and Democratic Transition

Historical Context of the Ideological Spectrum in Tunisia

The spread of ideologies in Tunisia has always been associated with the country's social and political development. Over the years, from its ancient Carthaginian foundations to modern times, the country has witnessed an upsurge of diverse streams of thought that have, in turn, shaped the country's national unity. Tunisia has always been a composite zone of juxtaposed and intertwined ideologies, from tribal customs and Islamic guidelines to colonial and modern political concepts. Today's Tunisia reflects the unrecognised lessons learnt from past struggles throughout its history. Tunisia has gone through an uninterrupted succession of events that have shaped its ideologies. These eras have served to change the ideological beliefs in the country. The pre-Islamic phase came with the settling of the native Berbers, the Roman occupants, and the Phoenicians, which changed the country and its ideologies forever. The Berbers and Phoenicians settled in Tunisia, forged ties with the Romans, and adopted nearly every single aspect of their culture over an expansive timeframe. Then came the period of colonial rule, which served to change the country's ideologies once more.

Tunisia experienced French colonial rule, which caused fractures in the existing societal norms and customs and introduced secular and Western ideas that fundamentally changed many aspects of the country. It was later during this period that the complex interaction between the Islamic heritage of the country, as well as secular modernity and the aspirations of national identity, developed. All of these had, at that time, affected the ideological divisions that still impact current Tunisia. The rest of the world viewed the struggle for independence as an opportunity for further ideological delineation and much-needed controversy. The nationalists appeared to introduce many ideas to the fabric of Tunisia, everything from the intricacies of Islam to the unfinished concepts of modern politics, socialism, and even pan-Arabism. During this period, the independence of Tunisia garnered attention for symbolising the union of various, often conflicting, Islamic ideas that aimed to create an inclusive identity. The overarching ideological past of Tunisia embodies what the country had to go through to traverse the diverse and complex phenomena that several other nations were enduring. Today, the struggle to preserve national unity, along with the "historical amnesia" that has recently been proposed by many, still reminds us that these phenomena are alive within the nation's political and social fabric.

Islamist Movements and Political Participation

Political developments in Tunisia have shown that Islamist organisations like Ennahda have garnered support and acceptance from some parts of the population because of the backing they have provided in favour of the accepted socio-political changes in the country. Since its establishment in 1981, Ennahda has maintained a relatively active presence in Tunisia. Ennahda is a clear example of an Islamist group in Tunisia that has transitioned from being in the political opposition to being an active participant following the political thaw in the country. Islamist movements in Tunisia have been, and still are, advocating for the application of Islamic guidelines to the country's politics, legislation, and social activities in an attempt to create a theocratic state. A country dominated by Islam is not a new phenomenon, and thus there have been discussions and, at times, heated controversies and disagreements. Islamist movements have been a key part of the country's politics and are often accused of working with the opposition. Since its emergence, and especially after the Arab Spring, Ennahda has been active in joining coalition governments, and this move has been the most controversial, as it has even divided Ennahda supporters in trying to prove that it is possible to be Islamist without imposing Islam on others. Ennahda's intra-party democracy suffers from divisions, sometimes to such an extent that it loses members. They represent the country's contradictions, and their presence has caused most of Tunisia's conflict.

The Arab Spring revolts arose as a pivotal moment for Islamist movements in Tunisia, as the Ennahda party gained considerable parliamentary presence following the country's revolution. These years saw heated debates concerning the intersection of governance and religion and the separation of church and state. The Islamist participation in the new constitutional framing exemplified their attempts to create a balance between Islamic law and integrative governance with a focus on human rights, which highlighted the underlying difficulties in addressing a spectrum of different ideological beliefs. Throughout all these events, the framing of Islamist sentiments and ambitions, and more importantly, their actual attempts at integration within the new governance structure have always faced the fiercest criticism. To grasp the complex nature of modern Tunisia and its new democratic challenges, it is equally important to ascertain the nature of participation by Islamist movements.

Secularism and Its Advocacy in National Discourse

While Tunisia's discussions have centred on secularism, which has influenced the country's politico-religious landscape, secularism has emerged as a response to the increasing need to separate governance from state religions and their associated theocratic constraints. Bourguiba's nation-building policies after independence and the positioning of secularism as a core principle of the state were part of his vision to modernise the country through the implementation of central legal and institutional reforms. Tunisia was the most progressive country in the region after the incorporation of the Personal Status Code in 1956, which almost single-handedly transformed the legal status of women by the grant of unprecedented rights and freedoms. Tunisia enjoyed wide-ranging support from the international community that sought to advance women's rights and affirm secularism. Like other North African and Middle Eastern countries that gained independence almost contemporaneously, Tunisia has also, from time to time, witnessed a revival and a slow but respectable embrace of secularism in the discourse of its people and its elite.

These orientations have had lapses, which have coincided with the acceptance of secularism. In addition to feelings of acknowledgement and pity, there have been efforts to unite in upholding cultural traditions, which have, I believe correctly, come to represent a form of patriotic vigilance. The most rigorous advocacy for the implementation of secularism, which aims to transform Tunisia into a modern nation-state by embracing Bourguiba's policies, has garnered critical support. Bourguiba operated within both the factual circumstances and the mythological narratives of government that articulate society's displacement, as expressed in foundational discourses.

In the juxtaposition of Bourguiba's counter-hegemonic efforts to disentangle the governance of a society's multiplicity of legal traditions centred on a national narrative of border articulation, the framing of Bourguiba as the universal other has been influenced by the transcendental myth of modernity.

This split has resulted in divided arguments that highlight the profound societal conflicts regarding the place of religion in society. In modern-day Tunisia, discussions concerning secularism seem almost synonymous with discussions regarding the country's identity and the protection of civil rights. The 2014 Constitution, hailed as one of the benchmarks of the country's democratic progress, contains provisions that attempt to guarantee the freedom of conscience and belief, as well as the neutrality of the state concerning religion, which are supposedly contradictory. Still, the constitutional provisions fuel ideological strife, and such strife can be observed in the conflicts over educational curricula, the public wearing of religious symbols, and the control of religious institutions. In the thick of these controversies, secular advocates urge the adoption of freedom-respecting, non-invasive policies that are geared toward religious practices, aiming for positive relations between the secular state and the various faith communities. This model attempts to balance the tenets of secular governance with the accommodation of pluralistic religious expressions in the public domain, which aims to emphasise respect for and understanding of one another. The secularism debate, even as Tunisia works toward consolidating democracy, remains crucial to the formation of a shared conception of national integration and social harmony.

Finding a middle ground between secularism and recognising different religions is an issue that can only be resolved with careful consideration, a negotiated settlement, and a commitment to protecting everyone's right to freedom.

Key Events Leading to Democratic Transition

A series of events characterised the democratic transition in Tunisia, significantly impacting the country's politics. One such turning point was the removal of President Zine El Abidine Ben Ali in January 2011, after the country had been subjected to protests largely due to economic burdens, political repression, and rampant corruption. The major turning point in Tunisia, called the Tunisian Revolution, the Jasmine Revolution, etc., is the one that instigated the rest of the Arab Spring. Following Ben Ali's departure, Tunisia had to undergo a very turbulent shift towards democracy. One major step towards this shift was the creation of the High Authority for the Achievement of the Objectives of the Revolution, Political Reform and Democratic Transition, usually referred to as the Higher Authority, which was instrumental in enabling Tunisia to undergo the necessary transformations. The sketching of a novel constitution and the organisation of free and fair elections, the first of their kind in the area, rest on the efforts of the Higher Authority and mark the beginnings of a more inclusive and democratic polity. January 2014 witnessed the most remarkable of the 2014 achievements, the adoption of the new constitution, which represents a decisive contribution to the democratic governance the country sorely lacks. The constitution accentuates the invaluable tenets of pluralism, human rights, and the governance of law and order, as well as the sensitive issue of the relationship between religion and the state. Its ratification indicated a joint undertaking of the different political forces of the country in fostering national dialogue and compromise as a means of achieving the much-needed national unity. The 2014 parliamentary and presidential elections, also won by the Tunisians, proved the determination of the populace to take their destiny into their hands and chart a course for the country's future. The elections were a contest for power among different political parties of various ideologies, which indicates the growing democratic ethos of the country. The ability of the different ideological groups to coexist, as well as the peaceful donation of power, demonstrates a further step in the consolidation of democratic norms within the country. The 2015 Nobel Peace Prize received by the Quartet, which was the first to award the national dialogue prize, was a mark of external appreciation for the collaboration that civil society organisations, trade unions, and employers' associations have devoted to averting political unrest and supporting consensus-building.

The award emphasised the need for dialogue and negotiations to manage ideology and avoid polarisation. The events that led to the transition to democracy in Tunisia highlight the country's ability and willingness to overcome self-inflicted fragmentation in the embrace of democratic ideals. These achievements created the basis of a more participatory and representative political order, which made Tunisia a shining example in a region plagued with instability.

Constitutional Debates: Religion and State

The constitutional debates, which concern the relationship between religion and the state in Tunisia, have been crucial to the evolution of the country's politics. Since its independence in 1956, Tunisia has transformed overwhelmingly in its secular and religious freedom policies. The period succeeding independence was characterised by state interference of all kinds in the religious sphere, where the government exercised control over her institutions and practices of religion. President Zine El Abidine Ben Ali's rule made this control clear by harshly cracking down on political Islam and Muslim institutions. The 2011 revolution ignited a fresh wave of democracy, prompting a thoughtful discussion about the role of religion in governance.

Slated to become one of the most important milestones to be remembered during these talks was the drafting of the constitution, a process that surely captured the clashes on the line of the place of religion in civil life. The resulting constitution upheld secularism principles and safeguarded religious freedom.

Major Actors and Ideological Alignment

Tunisia has social and political "theatres" where various actors perform distinct roles. Each actor in these 'theatres' represents different social and political ideologies – Islamism, secularism, and liberalism – and these ideologies, in social, political, economic, and class terms, are intertwined. There are various Ennahda Movements, which are the leading Islamist parties, and within these movements, members hold significant power in the country and its politics as they seek to integrate Islam into governance while also promoting democracy. On the other side, secularly influenced actors—for instance, Nidaa Tunis and secular Democrats—propose a system that promotes secularism and emphasises all kinds of freedoms and legal rights regardless of differences in religions. The aforementioned actors are the key participants in most ideological conflicts, which attract significant attention during the country's political changes.

The political fragmentation of Tunisia reflects ideological divisions within the landscape, which are analysed through a communications theory that identifies different levels of discourse on various subjects. Conflicts often diminish democracy's influence as various tribal factions strive to assert their power and vision for the country.

Impact of Ideological Divisions on Governance

Political fragmentation in Tunisia is influenced by ideological divisions within the landscape, which are analysed through a communication theory that identifies different levels of discourse on various subjects. Various tribal factions each attempt to impose their own power and vision for the country, leading to conflicts where democracy holds little influence and often disappears.

The lack of cohesion has stunted the ability to articulate and execute plans, thus resulting in perennial stagnation and decision-making paralysis during certain intervals. The cardinal differences in underlying principles and beliefs have also considerably weakened any chances of agreeing and formulating a compromise on paramount issues, stalling progress on the pivotal goals and undertakings of the initiatives and reforms. Ideological differences and multitudes of schools of thought have also added to the untold complexities in the disorder of the administration of the public domain, particularly by the manner in which the principles and strategies of appointment are tainted with the compromise of the prevailing ideological justifications and attachments, thus sidelining the abundant qualified personnel who are the antagonists of the dominating orthodox beliefs.

Public Sentiment and Ideological Expectations

The social attitudes in Tunisia, which are as diverse as they are engaging as a subject of study, are a product of a rich interplay of different expectations rooted traditionally, sociologically, and politically. Such multi-layered ideological configurations that Tunisia has seen have more or less been a reflex of the emotive tapestry of the Tunisian community. The complex emotions and public sentiments in Tunisia, representing a range of expectations, form the essence of social cohesion that must be understood to effectively address the argumentative multipolarities and ideological splits. Tunisian society is, on the one hand, unified, and on the other hand, to a significant extent, divided by differences and contrasts of sentiments and beliefs, with disjointed segments of society holding disparate beliefs on the conduct of governing, ethical standards, legal mores, and social order. The frictions and tensions that dominate the Tunisian socio-ideological landscape result in emerging ideological expectations, which form the fabric of social feelings and bring order out of chaos. The differences in people's attitudes towards religion, state power, and religion show complexity and layers in public sentiment. An appraisal suggests that there is a deep public appetite for stability, economic growth, and social justice. The differing ideological groups attach different values and policies to these goals. The Islamist stratum, for instance, underscores the dominance of religious values in the governance and policies of a state and stresses moral and cultural fundamentals to bring socio-political cohesion. The secularist faction, in turn, aligns their ideological aspirations with the variable of personal liberties, civil freedoms, and democracy, arguing for the separation of religion and politics and the advocacy of a pluralistic system. The divergent ideological positions constitute part of the complex matrix that society in general has, and these factors highlight the complexity of public attitude. Such sociopolitical stagnation and the desire to move forward construct a basic framework that public hopes and wishes stand upon. An evaluation of public sentiment also reveals the discontent of the public towards the functioning of the government, the character and reliability of its institutions, and the degree of respect for their basic liberties. The convergence and divergence of these ideological expectations highlight the nuanced aspirations of society, which suggest that deep contemplation and explanation are vital.

Shifting public opinion and ideological expectations are crucial to the direction of the debate and the resulting national policy. There is a critical need to appreciate the interaction between public opinion and the perceptions held at the ideological level, since the latter, and all the public policy implications that emanate from it, are crucial to the level of political agreement that can be reached and the resulting policy that can be put into place for the resulting cohesion in society. Examining aged public sentiment and ideological expectations requires a multi-level approach that considers social, spatial, and temporal dimensions. In this case, public opinion and sentiment reveal blind spots that must be addressed to understand how political traditions and discontinuities shape the construction of a national identity in Tunisia's historical record, educational system, and the diverse media that inform Tunisian society's ideological expectations.

In summary, the fragile nature of public opinion and the interconnectedness of public ideology indicate a need for inclusive discourse structures that promote direct and participatory democracy aimed at fostering reconciliation. Achieving reconciliation of divergent ideals and bridging the gap between people's perceptions is essential for the nation as it seeks deeper democracy and sustainable development.

Case Studies of Consensus Building

Before sustaining a pluralistic society, Tunisia engaged in several case studies in an attempt to build a consensus among conflicting ideological groups. One such case is the National Dialogue Quartet, which was instrumental in negotiations to end the 2013 political impasse. The quartet organised simultaneous discussions among the Tunisian General Labour Union, the Tunisian Confederation of Industry, Trade, and Handicrafts, the Tunisian Human Rights League, and the Tunisian Order of Lawyers and was able to keep open the pathways of communication between the disparate ideological representatives. The quartet's forceful negotiations and mediations positioned them positively within the contentious interests and competing priorities to earn a consensus that resulted in a technocratic government and a new constitution. This case demonstrates the opportunities for collaborative approaches in addressing ideological divides. The experience of the Ennahda Movement is even more remarkable. It transformed from an Islamist movement into a political party that embraced democratic participation, building alliances, and engaging in cross-party collaboration.

Seeking to close the gaps in understanding and to forge agreements with secular partners, Ennahda has demonstrated a willingness to engage in issue-based dialogue, pluralistic governance, and compromise. Furthermore, civil society actions, participants of Peace Clubs, and Interfaith Communities have served as small models of large-scale agreement fusions at the grassroots level, particularly in building trust and understanding across the divides of contrary beliefs and silos of contention. Their efforts exemplify the top-down strategies in building social agreement and cohesion. Finally, in international relations, the South African Truth and Reconciliation Commission and the Northern Ireland peace process post-conflict studies are invaluable regarding consensus-building after ideological conflicts through transitional, reconciliation, and post-conflict governance. Comparative reflection on these instances provides important grounding for the ongoing efforts of Tunisia. These models benefit Tunisia, and by incorporating their ideas, Tunisia is able to fortify its cooperative goals rooted in pluralism.

Looking Forward: Bridging Ideological Gaps for Unity

It is important that Tunisia, in its vision for the country and situation, devises strategies to close the ideological gaps that exist among the citizens.

Achieving this goal requires cross-sectional collaboration among all participants. First and foremost, there is a pressing need to resolve the standoff between Islamists and secularists. Such conversations need to take place based on grounds of civility and the goal of reaching consensus and sympathy on both sides. Furthermore, patriotism through the education system is at the forefront of constructing a unifying national identity. Schools with comprehensive curricula that embrace diverse views and ideologies essential for nation-building inadvertently promote a limited understanding of citizenship. In addition, the field of media itself is also important because it can contribute to ideological and social fragmentation and polarisation or help resolve them. Supporting and promoting social responsibility in journalism and restrictive policies based on the underlying media thesis of extremism can redress the imbalance in public opinion about "full freedom". Furthermore, policies for economic growth and wider social inclusion must overcome ideological divisions to resolve underlying grievances. Increasing economic opportunities for all citizens, therefore, can help Tunisia integrate citizenship and inclusively eliminate the divisive socioeconomic fault lines that heighten ideological division. In particular, self-governing community rounds that bring together participants of different orientations for cooperative work and social activities can help eliminate social intergroup hostilities.

Reconciliation and transitional justice processes rest on historical grievances and traumas, which start ideological rifts and divisions in a society. For a more cohesive and reconciled society, offer processes of truth-telling, apology, and healing. Closing the ideological gaps in Tunisia will rest on the ongoing efforts of the government, civil society, religious leaders, and the citizens as a whole. This unity-building process will need time and a lot of empathy and resilience towards the challenges faced. It requires a vision much deeper than political rhetoric and much longer than the election cycle for the common welfare of the country. Tunisia has the opportunity to embrace democracy and inclusiveness as foundational in the political realm, which will enable the country to address the challenges of unity and division in society.

References For Further Reading

Historical Context of the Ideological Spectrum

1. Perkins, K. (2014). A History of Modern Tunisia (2nd ed.). Cambridge University Press.
2. Abdallah, S. (2018). The Colonial Legacy in Tunisia: Fractured Society, Divided Politics. The Journal of North African Studies, 23(3), 511-515.
3. Hermassi, A. (1972). Leadership and National Development in North Africa. University of California Press.

Islamist Movements and Political Participation

4. McCarthy, R. (2018). Re-thinking Secularism in Post-Independence Tunisia. Oxford University Press.
5. Cavatorta, F., & Merone, F. (2013). Moderation through Exclusion? The Journey of the Tunisian Ennahda from Fundamentalist to Conservative Party. Democratization, 20(5), 857-875.
6. Wolf, A. (2017). Ennahda's Identity Crisis and the Future

of Tunisian Democracy. The Washington Institute for Near East Policy.

Secularism, Bourguiba, and the Personal Status Code

7. Charrad, M. M. (2001). States and Women's Rights: The Making of Postcolonial Tunisia, Algeria, and Morocco. University of California Press.
8. Mahfoudh, D., & Mahfoudh, A. (2014). Social Movements and the Question of Leadership: The Case of the Tunisian Feminist Movement. Revue des Mondes Musulmans et de la Méditerranée, 135, 55-72.

Democratic Transition, Constitution, and Consensus Building

9. Marks, M. (2014). Convince, Coerce, or Compromise? Ennahda's Approach to Tunisia's Constitution. Brookings Institution.
10. International Crisis Group. (2014). Tunisia: Transitional Justice and the Fight Against Corruption. Middle East and North Africa Report No. 168.
11. Bellin, E. (2020). The Jasmine Revolution and the Paradox of Governance in Tunisia. In Political Science Quarterly, 135(1), 123-155.

Key Actors, Governance, and Public Sentiment

12. Gana, N. (Ed.). (2013). The Making of the Tunisian Revolution: Contexts, Architects, Prospects. Edinburgh University Press.
13. Ayari, M. B. (2016). The Unfinished Revolution of Dignity: The Struggle for Power and Identity in Tunisia. The Carnegie Endowment for International Peace.
14. The Tunisian National Dialogue Quartet. (2015). Nobel Peace Prize Award Ceremony Speech.

Looking Forward: Bridging Ideological Gaps

15. Benstead, L. J. (2018). Why Do Some Arab Citizens See Democracy as Unsuitable for Their Country? Comparative Political Studies, 51(14), 1933-1965.
16. United Nations Development Programme (UNDP). (2022). The Future of Social Contract in Tunisia: Rethinking the State-Citizen Relationship. UNDP Tunisia.

9
Regional Comparisons
Why Tunisia Stands Apart

Regional Dynamics

The Maghreb nations—Morocco, Algeria, Tunisia, Libya, and Mauritania—each with distinct political and economic systems and diverse cultures that have common colonial and post-colonial histories, also have deeply intertwined and complex geopolitical, historical, and cultural systems. It is, therefore, no surprise that these countries formed strong collective and distinct identities while establishing intricate interrelations with each other and other countries. In addition to these countries being renowned for their historical colonialism and their struggles for independence, the crossroads they establish between the Mediterranean Sea and the rest of the world enable easy access to major global trade routes, migration, and, unfortunately, military and commercial antagonism, making their geopolitical significance even more important. From a social perspective, the numerous ethnic groups and their languages and religions—each with their sets of governance problems—add further governance and diplomatic relations complications.

Everything previously stated indicates that the geopolitical landscape of North Africa, and more specifically the interconnections of these nations, requires particular attention and analysis. Only by assessing the historical foundations, contemporary issues, and future trajectories of the Maghreb countries can we approach such an analysis. This examination will also provide an understanding of the growing interconnections of these countries with other global nations and the international consequences that ensue from these relations.

Historical Contextualisation of Maghreb Nations

The Maghreb region, which includes Tunisia, Algeria, Morocco, Libya, and Mauritania, is characterised by a diverse and intricate history that has greatly influenced the political, social, and cultural landscapes of these countries.

Occupying a geographical vantage point between Europe and Africa and bordering the Mediterranean Sea, the Maghreb region consists of five countries: Morocco, Algeria, Tunisia, Libya, and Mauritania. Morocco and the Mauritanian southern border shield the region from extreme climatic conditions. Therefore, Morocco, Spain, Algeria, Tunisia, and Libya benefit from the favourable geography of the Maghreb. Its geographical position has always attracted the attention of several civilisations, which led to the development of trade. The proximity to Europe and the Mediterranean enhances its strategic importance. Maghreb is often called a crescent of Islam. The onset of the second wave of Islamization gave the Maghreb a more profound consolidation as a crossroads of Islamic civilisation. The term "Arch of Islam" often refers to the significant expansion of the Maghreb and its role in uniting the Islamic empire across Europe and Africa. The Maghreb region has always been of great interest to the civilisations of the Mediterranean due to its favourable natural resources and commercial potential. The region is still of tremendous importance due to its strategic position and Islamic civilisation heritage.

Nevertheless, the incursions of the Arabs and Islam did

not completely obliterate the Berber character and social systems already in place. Instead, this blending of Arab and Berber cultures and customs defines Maghrebi culture. The following centuries brought European incursions, particularly from the Spanish, Portuguese, and French, each of which left permanent marks on the Maghreb's history. The imposition of colonial rule altered the region's Maghreb governance, control, economic structures, and even cultural systems, which has left legacies felt in present Maghrebi society to this day. The mid-20th century marks the period of loss of colonial rule and the freedom struggles, whereby these countries sought to regain their national identity and sovereignty. The historical context of the Maghreb countries demonstrates the interconnectedness of their histories and underscores their unique development paths. The intricate histories of these countries, in particular the Maghreb, help to understand the realities of these countries today and the reason for the peculiar case of Tunisia in the region.

Political Systems – A Comparative Analysis

Political Systems: The political systems of the Maghreb region have never been analysed, and Tunisia has also never been contrasted with its regional neighbours or valued for its singular governance system and processes. The legacy of colonial rule, post-independence struggles, and current geopolitical conditions have also shaped the political systems of Algeria, Morocco, Libya, and Mauritania. All systems of governance within this region may bear resemblance to one another culturally and historically, but the political advancement in each nation has produced vastly different outcomes. Algeria, for instance, exhibits a legacy of central control with a dominant executive branch and military rule, making it a semi-presidential republic. In comparison, Morocco is a constitutional monarchy, but the executive, elected representatives, and parliamentary systems of governance function in intricate tandem. In Libya, the fall of the Gaddafi regime has precipitated severe political instability, giving rise to fractured governance and skirmishes among competing factions. Mauritania is a curious case; its history of military coups is belied by the nation's current status as a presidential republic with a system of executive and legislative parliamentary mechanisms. Unlike the other Maghreb countries, Tunisia underwent an exceptional transformation post-independence, after which it embraced multiparty democracy and embarked on the separation of powers and other institutional reforms.

Tunisia's installation of a semi-presidential system along with a modern constitution that features civil liberties and pluralism makes it distinct in the Maghreb region. Tunisia's unique political system has enabled it to overcome transition, maintain democracy, and promote inclusive governance. Additionally, Tunisia's successful transition to democracy and its consensus-based politics have isolated the country in the region because of the differing experiences of its neighbours. In addition, the polarisation and absence of civic engagement that have characterised the rest of the Maghreb do not fully explain the vibrant civil society, advocacy groups, and labour organisations in Tunisia that have strengthened its democracy. Tunisia's exceptional political dynamics that include the ability of non-state actors to influence policymakers and account for the institutions are profoundly unique to the region. In conclusion, the differences in political systems justify Tunisia's exceptionalism within the Maghreb region.

Through democratic governance and constitutional reform, coupled with systematic civic engagement, Tunisia is the most manifest expression of political pluralism and inclusive decision-making and thus provides a model for the rest of North Africa.

Socioeconomic Indicators and Development Trajectories

Tunisia's socioeconomic conditions and indicators of development provide an intriguing story of progress and stagnation in the evolution of the country. Understanding key indicators such as GDP growth, unemployment, inequitable income distribution, and state of poverty creates a picture of Tunisia's economy. Tunisia's socioeconomic development witnessed the gleichschaltung of great progress with stagnation, and Tunisia has certainly gone through its more-than-impressive eras in the past decades. Watershed decisions and domestic reforms shaped by external and internal forces have dominated Tunisia's modern economic history. In the post-independence phase, the state adopted a mixed economy as a model for development and instituted government intervention, with a preeminent focus on industrialisation. It pioneered success in agriculture, tourism, and then in manufacturing, which in turn contributed to the overall economic development of the country. It has suffered from a myriad of industry and governance issues due to the lack of a more reliable, resilient and diversified economy. In addition, external economic shocks and regional instability have hindered its growth and contributed to stagnation.

The 2011 Arab Spring uprisings were the beginning of numerous calls for political change and social and economic justice. While the revolution was a landmark event for Tunisia, it also created confusion and interruptions for the country's growing path. In the following years, there was a change in the volume of investments, economic policies, and shifts in trade relations, all of which were Tunisia's means of gauging progress on various social and economic indicators. Tunisia's capacity to integrate complexities and create pathways for sustainable progress in the past few years is commendable. Foreign investment and competitiveness enhancement form the foundation of Tunisia's development agenda. More importantly, developmental efforts that seek to address youth, gender, and regional inequalities have all, in one way or another, aimed to make progress towards inclusive and equitable development. Education and skill enhancement programmes have emerged with the purpose of preparing the population for a knowledge-driven economy. Tunisia's development path, marked with intractable issues like high youth unemployment, regional inequality, and the predominance of the informal economy, is complex. Tunisia's development is also a reflection of the prescribed approaches accompanied by considerable governance as well as strategic foresight and planning. Further, Tunisia's sustainable development and future progress rely on much more creative and entrepreneurial approaches with rational resource use.

In the present-day world, Tunisia grapples with the challenges of socioeconomic advancement alongside the protection of its socio-cultural legacy, thus informing the goals and objectives of the country in a complex and interwoven international order.

Cultural and Religious Influences on Governance

The decreased threshold mentioned above formulates the parameters of all aspects of rule; Tunisia, hosting a unique combination of legacies, traditions, and modern interpretations of Islam, offers a case in point. Tunisia's historical position at the centre of marketplace exchange on the Mediterranean Sea shaped it into an oasis of different cultures and peoples; the standards and values of society were, in turn, affected by Phoenician, Roman, Arabic, and Berber civilisations. The social tapestry of the superimposed cultures also moulded the governance, and several folk customs are still active in the 'decision-making'. Islam, binding Tunisia, is still a principal and guiding social fact and, thus, a predominant aspect of the legal system, moral codes, and social obligations.

Moreover, the various interpretations of Islam within Tunisian society have sparked intricate discussions about the connections between religion and politics, with various groups supporting differing degrees of theocracy. This variety of points of view has resulted in a vigorous and shifting conversation about the role of religion in public life, which has further complicated the tapestry of Tunisia's governance. Nonetheless, Tunisia also has a robust tradition of secularism, which has historically acted as a shield against the clergy's undue intervention into the country's governance. This intricate amalgam of religious and secular elements of government has been a hallmark of Tunisia's political landscape, conferring a distinctive form of governance unlike that of its neighbours. Understanding Tunisia's governance system in its entirety is to acknowledge and engage with these cultural and religious elements of governance. With this engaged deconstruction, we can understand the historical discontinuities and complexities that characterise the country's political system and, subsequently, attempt to establish more equitable and integrative governance that honours the country's profound cultural and vivid spiritual tapestry.

Civil Society and Pluralism in Tunisia

Recognised in the region for its distinctive character, Tunisian civil society is the product of many years of grassroots activism, coupled with the work of numerous non-governmental organisations. Tunisian civil society also marks the strides made by the country towards the cultivation of governance pluralism, democratically and inclusively. Immediately after the country's independence, numerous advocacy, human rights, and professional organisations sprang up, seeking to serve various interests. Their actions demonstrated civic responsibility and dedication to the democratic process. These organisations have immensely contributed to the democratic practice of the country by fostering public discourse, advocating for changes to some government policies, and monitoring government activities. The pluralism of Tunisian civil society is clear from the inclusion of women's groups, the practitioners of civic and culture, and the environment. The multiplicity of actions taken speaks to the power of activism by or in support of the oppressed. The overwhelming majority of the population in Tunisia, the region's model of largely homogeneous neighbourhoods, respects and promotes community and interethnic dialogue. Tunisia has long taken pride in its social inclusion, a country that traditionally resolves quarrels without remorse. Talking about peaceful cooperation, Tunisia takes a region-wide model position with the rest of the world.

While heading off in different directions and dealing with diverse issues, Tunisian civil society has integrated and adopted evolving needs through the creation and use of digital platforms and social media to promote collective action, factor advocacy, and the practice of democratic values. In addition, collaboration with foreign institutions and transnational networks has resulted in the cross-border exchange of knowledge, capacity-building, and collaboration in the fields of human development and peace-building. Through these collaborations, Tunisian civil society has demonstrated its ability to address issues such as inequality, transitional justice, and humanitarian concerns in a deep and reflective manner. Having such an approach is an added value in the social problems Tunisia has to confront.

The ecosystem supporting civil society in Tunisia results from a socio-legal context that allows the populace to develop bottom-up and people-led initiatives. Nevertheless, with continuing unresolved deep-seated structural issues such as red tape, civil society is unable to fully achieve its potential. To overcome these obstacles, robust networking must occur both vertically and horizontally among state actors, civil society, and the international arena to ensure that civil society can fully develop and make an impact. Improving processes and public service, along with increasing financial resources, will permit Tunisia to democratically grow its civil society, which will enable robust participation in the country's development efforts.

Security Challenges and Regional Stability

Tunisia, as the central country in the Maghreb region, has to face different security problems which arise in the region and have relevance for its stability.

Tunisia's location next to Libya and Algeria has consistently created a special set of geopolitical challenges, particularly in light of the recent political and military unrest experienced by both nations. The conflict in Libya has also led to an influx of migrants and refugees into Tunisia, putting significant strain on the country's infrastructure and resources. The internal landscape, on the other hand, has been shaped by increasing tensions between armed non-state and extremist movements on the peripheries bordering Tunisia and in the mostly ignored socio-economically deprived regions. The state's response to the situation remains contentious, considering balancing the use of excessive force and respecting the fundamental freedoms of the dissenting citizens. Tunisia's persisting municipal and regional conflicts have, hand in hand, brought the legacy of authoritarianism into the picture, which is especially revealing in the state's relationship with its own civil society and individual liberty, security, and social order. Beyond its economically orientated regional activity, Tunisia has been able to establish its international ties at a more advanced level than its basic bilateral ties. Tunisia is committed to multilateral frameworks to foster international cooperation and strengthen the country's security and regional peace.

Tunisia's active participation in international security initiatives, including joint military training, intelligence sharing, and collaboration on counter-terrorism efforts, still has more to cover. Apart from conventional security concerns, Tunisia's geographical location also exposes it to environmental and socio-economic disadvantages. The impacts of climate change, such as desertification and water scarcity, pose resource-based national and regional security challenges. Moreover, imbalances in social equity and economic opportunity can increase social tension and unrest, thus threatening the stability of the entire Maghreb region. Tunisia's security challenges are multi-layered. Therefore, the response has to be integrated. These include strengthening the border, institution building, improving surveillance and community policing, and inclusive political frameworks. These, among others, will bilaterally improve regional stability. For Tunisia to maintain its favourable geopolitical position, it will need a comprehensive security strategy that responds to both regional and global challenges, as well as cross-cutting internal and external dynamics. Tunisia's position within the region will also significantly enhance the Maghreb's stability.

Economic Alliances and Trade Dependencies

Tunisia's economic alliances and trade dependencies are crucial to the country's socio-economic profile.

Tunisia has been able to establish strong partnerships around the world due to its geopolitical location at the intersection of Europe, Africa, and the Middle East. Tunisia has been able to advance its economic policies and trade relations because of its membership. Tunisia has improved relations within the Euro-Mediterranean Partnership and the AMU, which in turn has enhanced the industrial and agricultural sectors due to increased market access and foreign investments. While participating in both regional and global agreements on trade and investment, Tunisia has focused on fostering economic investment cooperation in the context of diversified partnerships. This, in turn, has improved economic and technological cooperation at bilateral and multilateral levels. Tunisia's status as an exporter has improved economic cooperation and reduced trade barriers, allowing it to meet all its goals. Tunisia also values cooperation in services and goods for economic development and job creation. Once again, Tunisia has improved relations with regional partners such as Algeria and Morocco, which has enhanced intra-regional collaboration and economic integration. Tunisia has been able to serve as a transcontinental bridge for trade, and the nation has improved its position as a North African economic centre due to its enhanced regional geopolitical situation.

The previously mentioned global partnerships and interdependence create both advantages and obstacles at the same time. Fluctuations within the global arena, as well as market variations and potential geopolitical conflicts, may, however, have ramifications for Tunisia's economy. Therefore, the primary goal of these France-Tunisia domestic and foreign policies is to bolster Tunisia's economic stability and safeguard it against external shocks.

With respect to foreign policies, the level of autonomy afforded to Tunisia as a trading partner in the region serves as a solid basis for growing international trade. If Tunisia, however, does not align the principles of sustainability with international trade policies, the economic constituency of the country risks isolating it diplomatically, xenophobically, and through eco-critical policies that strongly parallel the interests of foreign stakeholders. The trade objectives and policies of Tunisia have to correspond to the economic constituents, which can be achieved by examining the complex web of trade agreements Tunisia has signed. To achieve international economic objectives, Tunisia can establish a well-integrated deep-sea port that adheres to global standards.

Social Policies and Human Rights Advancements

An analysis of the social policies and human rights of Tunisia demonstrates how much the country has changed. When President Ben Ali was removed from office, Tunisia started systematic changes to turn the country around and alleviate social abuse as well as ameliorate governance. As part of the changes to help the country economically, the government started making and modifying policies to strengthen human rights, like the 'Women and Gender Law' and the 'Truth and Dignity Commission', to provide justice and rectify discrimination. These initiatives aim to restructure Tunisia's disintegrating social coexistence, promoting inclusion and social tolerance. Tunisia was also the first Arab country to attain social justice alongside the preservation of international laws and various bilateral pacts. Tunisia has also made remarkable changes in the international programmes designed to alleviate inequity, social exclusion, and poverty, which has made inroads into the policies needed to build a supportive social system. Provision of social services, education, healthcare, and housing are key pillars of the raised living conditions.

Moreover, the recognition and incorporation of minority groups into the national framework have demonstrated Tunisia's efforts toward greater societal fairness and pluralism. Even with these gains, challenges remain, particularly regarding the rights of workers, the rights to free speech, and the rights of the LGBTQ+ community. Addressing these gaps will be critical to further advancing Tunisia's social policies and the state of human rights in the country. Tunisia's approach to democratic governance, and the accompanying social changes, will have to balance these growing trends with the human rights gaps to preserve the country's unique position in the region.

Conclusion – The Path Forward for Tunisia's Distinctiveness

Tunisia must maintain its unique position at the intersection of history and modernity. It will have to answer the question of how to deploy this uniqueness on multiple fronts. Tunisia's human rights record, particularly the social policies emphasised in the region, shows a country capable of progressive governance and development. We should also highlight the country's pluralistic and inclusive policies. The full inclusion of every citizen, along with the protection of their rights, will bolster the democracy of the country and act as a guiding light for other countries in the area confronting the same issues. The case of Tunisia offers important insights regarding the balance between modernity and tradition and serves as a model for social peace and bridges in Tunisian pluralistic society. The ability to strengthen its market will drive the country's sustained growth and prosperity from a competitiveness and innovation perspective. Tunisia has the potential to become a trade and investment centre in the region with the right vision and prudent economic policies, leveraging its unique strengths as a highly integrated global economy. Unrestricted economic growth and growth in the workforce are essential in promoting Tunisians from all walks of life and empowering the country to become self-sufficient. With the growing security concerns in the region, Tunisia's efforts to maintain stability and counter-terrorism remain equally important.

Through constructive partnership frameworks with like-minded countries to address mutual security challenges, Tunisia can exert its power as a stabiliser and simultaneously strengthen its defences against external threats. To sum up, the remarkable determination and fortitude that Tunisia showed with the way they dealt with the historical burdens and modern-day challenges is a testament to the exceptionalism of this nation. If Tunisia pursues the pathway defined in this chapter, the country will still be on a trajectory that promotes continued advancement, growth, and sociability, not just as a pillar of North Africa but also as a source of guidance and inspiration well beyond its borders.

References For Further Reading

Regional Dynamics & Historical Contextualisation

1. Willis, M. J. (2012). Politics and Power in the Maghreb: Algeria, Tunisia and Morocco from Independence to the Arab Spring. Hurst & Company.
2. Entelis, J. P. (Ed.). (1997). Islam, Democracy, and the State in North Africa. Indiana University Press.
3. Vandewalle, D. (2012). A History of Modern Libya. Cambridge University Press.

Political Systems – A Comparative Analysis

4. Storm, L. (2014). Party Politics and the Prospects for Democracy in North Africa. Lynne Rienner Publishers.
5. Heydemann, S. (Ed.). (2004). Networks of Privilege in the Middle East: The Politics of Economic Reform Revisited. Palgrave Macmillan.

Socioeconomic Indicators and Development Trajectories

6. World Bank. (2020). The Unfinished Revolution: Bringing Opportunity, Good Jobs and Greater Wealth to All Tunisians. World Bank Group.

7. Achy, L. (2011). Tunisia's Economic Challenges. The Carnegie Endowment for International Peace.

Cultural and Religious Influences on Governance

8. Charrad, M. M. (2001). States and Women's Rights: The Making of Postcolonial Tunisia, Algeria, and Morocco. University of California Press.

9. Zeghal, M. (2008). Islamism in the Shadow of the State: Religion and Politics in Morocco and Tunisia. In Politics & Society, 36(1), 123-149.

Civil Society and Pluralism in Tunisia

10. Hawthorne, A. (Ed.). (2005). Is Civil Society the Answer? The Role of Civil Society in the Middle East and North Africa. The Carnegie Endowment for International Peace.

11. Beissinger, M., Jamal, A., & Mazur, K. (2015). Explaining Divergent Revolutionary Coalitions: Regime Strategies and the Structuring of Participation in the Tunisian and Egyptian Revolutions. Comparative Politics, 48(1), 1-24.

Security Challenges and Regional Stability

12. Lutterbeck, D. (2013). Migrants, Weapons and Oil: Europe and Libya after the Arab Spring. The Journal of North African Studies, 18(2), 275-293.
13. Boukhars, A. (2016). The Geography of Arab Protest: Taking the Revolution to the Peripheries. The Carnegie Endowment for International Peace.

Economic Alliances and Trade Dependencies

14. European Commission. (2021). EU-Tunisia Association Agreement: Deepening Trade Relations.
15. Draper, P. (2012). Breaking Free from Europe: Why Africa Needs Another Model of Regional Integration. The South African Institute of International Affairs.

Social Policies and Human Rights Advancements

16. Mullin, C., & Tozan, A. (2019). The Politics of Transitional Justice in Tunisia: Innovation, Continuity and Impact. The Journal of North African Studies, 24(5), 691-714.
17. Human Rights Watch. (Annual). World Report: Tunisia.

10
The Future of Tunisian Exceptionalism
Contemporary Challenges and Institutional Resilience

Contemporary Context

To appreciate the contemporary context of Tunisia, it is necessary to consider the most recent developments in the country's socio-political sphere, which undoubtedly will be important for the direction Tunisia is going to take in the future. Tunisia is experiencing socio-political, economic, and structural changes; therefore, understanding these changes will be important when predicting the country's future direction. In every revolution, the emerging governance structure is often significantly influenced by its predecessor; in Tunisia's case, this influence manifests as an attempt to extend democratic principles. It is clear from the Tunisia case that the growing youth population has heightened demands for more economic and political leverage, which has transformed the politics and governance of the country. Additionally, the influence of regional and global geopolitical factors makes Tunisia's global positioning increasingly significant. Tunisia's ability to analyse its contemporary socio-political features will offer a more profound understanding of how the country navigates changes in the political landscape and the strategies it aims to implement. Studying the potential of Tunisia will provide researchers an improved understanding of the impact that socio-political changes will have on its prospects.

Political Landscape: Evolving Governance Structures

Much has changed in the political landscape of the country regarding governance systems since the 2011 revolution. The desire to construct an enduring democracy that is open, accountable, and participatory has primarily fuelled this shift. The most prominent of such changes is the restructuring of the executive, legislative, and judicial systems for the purposes of fostering mutual control and diminishing the concentration of power. The years following the revolution saw the breakdown of the authoritarian system and simultaneous construction of a new constitutional order. This period, described in such a way, marks a new epoch in the system of governance, imbued with changes of an overwhelming degree. To this end, the focus has been on the decentralisation and devolution of power to the local level to stimulate the involvement of citizens and local governance. In addition, the birth of political pluralism and the development of various political and interest groups and their parties created a demand for interparty and intergroup coalitions and consensus decision-making. All of these factors have served to change political discussions and debates to encourage a culture of dialogue and compromise.

Furthermore, the evolution of governance has placed an emphasis on the redress of inequities and the promotion of social justice. The government has aimed to construct policies and institutions that respond to the needs of the disadvantaged and bridge socio-economic gaps. In addition to these policies, there has been a greater focus on improving the rights of women, youth, and other groups that are less fortunate. This process has made democracy and social justice even stronger. Also, critical within the context of the changing governance frameworks is the ongoing collaboration with civil society and the advocacy for the governance of the people. The collaboration of civil society with the state in the formulation and execution of policies is fundamental in ensuring that the people's needs and problems are substantially addressed. The promotion of human rights, democracy, ethical governance, and environmental care by civil society has been the most dominant factor contributing positively to the political situation of the country. The commitment to construct resilient structures of governance is fundamental as Tunisia attempts to resolve the complexities of its political transition. It means deepening the achievements of democratisation, strengthening the law, and increasing institutional capacity to confront external shocks.

Navigating through challenges and opportunities for stable and effective governance also requires constant planning and responsiveness to the needs of sidelined societal elements, such as Tunisia.

Economic Resilience in a Globalised Market

Tunisia has engaged with the new global economy in all its opportunities and complexities. Tunisia, concentrating on economic resilience, diversifies its industries and resources to adapt, survive, and prosper in an intensely competitive global economy. Tunisia's economic policy seeks to promote competitive innovation while enhancing sustainable development. Dynamic growth in agriculture, tourism, and information and communication technology, as well as manufacturing industries, has enabled the country to grow its economy and to attract foreign direct investment. Tunisia aims to deploy the Digital Economy and Society 2020 Initiative and other technology instruments to enhance productivity. Tunisia has improved its infrastructure and its financial, regulatory, and business regimes to ease the flow of business and trade. Tunisia's commitment to a diverse economy means trade diversification, new trade group partnerships, and the export promotion of volatile commodities, which all ensure stability and reduce risks. Involvement in human capital development and prudent government spending tells a great deal about Tunisia's intentions to prepare its citizens to tackle the realities of the global economy. Education and skills development positively correlate to the health of the economy, as sustainable economic development will only come from a republic whose citizens are responsive to change.

Moreover, with the promotion of entrepreneurship and innovation initiatives, there is a vibrant startup ecosystem, enhanced imagination, and a new growth-orientated thrust of the economy. Tunisia also recognises the need for social development and environmental protection. The country intends to alleviate the adverse impacts of economic development through its strategic plans for sustainable environmental management and the promotion of renewable energies and sustainable growth using protective measures. Tunisia is working on a detailed plan to strengthen its economy, allowing it to handle the challenges of the global market and seize new growth opportunities, ensuring its long-term success and stability.

Societal Dynamics and Urbanisation Trends

While Tunisia has had to grapple with the guise of modernity, understanding the phenomenon of urbanisation is important. The country has experienced continued population growth in urban areas, and the population density in the cities has been rising. Urbanisation has far-reaching impacts, like the shifts and changes of social structures like family and culture and changes in civic attitudes. The migration of people from rural areas to urban centres has led to overcrowding in cities, characterised by poorly constructed settlements, inadequate housing, insufficient infrastructure, and poor resource management— all of which are common issues in developing countries.

This development of cities has forced people to analyse clouding issues like the provision of primary services, the lack of sufficient jobs, and the major system of inequality through the lens of socio-economic development within a region.

Technological Advancements and Digital Integration

Technology and the internet's role have been fundamental to the transformation of modern-day Tunisia. Over the past few years, Tunisia has demonstrated an ever-increasing ability to use technology for innovation, connectivity, and to stimulate economic growth. Tunisia has aggressively deployed digital technology, whether it is through the development of a nationwide digitised infrastructure or e-commerce and other global internet trading platforms. The educational system has also seen success and advancement in this digital era, particularly through the use of artificial intelligence tools like ChatGPT. Teachers and students alike have been able to adopt this technology in an enchanting way and to build exciting and productive digital educational environments in which both groups can gain maximum benefits. Additionally, the global competitive market has compelled Tunisia to train and deploy a rapidly growing digital workforce to support it. This trend is also evident in the development of technology parks, incubators, and vibrant start-up ecosystems, which the government has built to foster the rate of technological entrepreneurship and innovation.

From fintech and agri-tech to healthcare and renewable energy, the entrepreneurial spirit has pioneered innovative solutions to challenges in every industry. The Tunisian entrepreneurial ecosystem has creatively harnessed new technologies to accentuate the disruptive and constructive waves of innovation and sustainable development. Alongside these transformations, the government's digitisation of service delivery and administrative processes has removed layers of red tape, improved administrative transparency, and increased public confidence. E-governance and digital citizen engagement tools allow the government's willingness to share power to reinforce participation and accountability in a democracy to lower the barriers to public engagement. The fusion of technology and governance has enabled the more streamlined delivery of public services and improved policy decisions. Technology and digitalisation in Tunisia have a lot of promise for the future. The new Tunisia, equipped with innovation, digital literacy, and technology, can adopt proper tools and techniques to enhance its engagement with the driving forces of globalisation and nurture its much-valued distinctive cultural traditions while enhancing the global mosaic of technology.

Environmental Challenges and Sustainable Solutions

The environmental setting of Tunisia cultivates many issues arising from the effects of climate change, including the contours of climate change, water scarcity, and loss of biodiversity—all of which Tunisia has come to face. Tunisia is undoubtedly exposed to the previously mentioned issues, as the elevations and temperatures, shifts of rain, and the intensity of excruciating climate events have shown tendencies to grow. Tunisia faces significant challenges due to its desert climate, which has always threatened cultivable land and tends to worsen food scarcity. A desert climate reduces agricultural productivity and has the potential to displace people from rural areas, which in turn increases their economic burdens. Scarcity of water is another of the issues faced by Tunisia as a result of the unregulated tapping of subsurface waters. The constantly growing population also contributes to the issue. The loss of the world's biodiversity, and Tunisia in particular, is a byproduct of unregulated burning of the land, uncontrolled land activities, and the development of cities. If we want to preserve various ecosystems, countermeasures should be raised. A sufficient number of regulations and balanced measures are necessary to conserve local wildlife and implement reinforced methods that prevent access to neglected urbanised areas. We can conclude that Tunisia needs to address issues in the country from many angles and focus on environmental integrity.

The promotion of adaptive agricultural practices using afforestation, along with the development of technologies for sustainable water use, directly contributes to soil conservation and desertification control. Strategically, the adoption of more controlled water usage regulations, combined with water savings technologies, water storage facility improvements, and desalination technologies, can slow the pace of water scarcity and stress in densely populated urban centres and rural areas. Public awareness, education, and active participation are vital to the culture of sustainable development and broad environmental protection advocacy. The first steps in sustainable development in Tunisia include strengthening environmental governance and freedom, as well as enacting and effectively enforcing sustainable development laws, environmental protective laws, and pro-sustainable eco initiatives. In this regard, the most important consequences of Tunisia's environmental proposition are the most sustainable policies. Effective practices to stabilise the country's water shortage issues, in addition to desalination, will advance the country's global geopolitical leadership. Achievements in trusted leadership and transformative change will position Tunisia to lead the global conversation about balancing biodiversity and socio-economic growth with sustainable leadership and global ecosystems.

This focus will ensure the country's transformative water scarcity issues are vertically integrated to support the ecosystem. It will shift focus beyond water efficiency and protection to harness the country's vast spatial opportunities and the country's natural sink for sustainable agriculture. We will enumerate the initiatives aimed at developing the knowledge economy, the systematic changes, the impediments, and the global geopolitical position in the context of Tunisia's strategic role. Sustainable leadership, transformative trust, and water positivity will advance geopolitical integrations. Tunisia will take a leading role at the intersection of ecosystems and soil management. There is a need for practical workforce training to meet the demands of the global market. Educational infrastructure is also important because it supports improvement and innovative thinking. Such training is particularly important for the retention of the country in the global market.

Education Reform and Knowledge Economy

There exists a contradiction in the achievements and struggles of the Tunisian education system. Although the majority of people now have access to primary and secondary education, the system's capacity to offer a comprehensive and pertinent curriculum still needs improvement. Educational commuters are deemed crucial in relation to the growing industries and technological change. Graduates in the contemporary world need competencies relevant to the present.

Graduates need to be as competitive as the job market dictates. There are imbalances in the education opportunities in the urban and rural areas of the country. These are some of the barriers to the education resources in the country. In addition to the infrastructure strides, retention policies for the teachers are crucial. This process entails heavy investment in the people working in the deprived areas. Investment in education will mitigate innovation and creativity deficits among citizens.

There already exists a framework for investing in youth with the intent of expanding the country towards a knowledge economy. This shift entails a change in the country's economy from the traditional primary industries to a knowledge-focused economy. If the country doesn't take these steps, it risks falling behind in the face of global shifts.

Joint innovative approaches to curriculum development in educational institutions and industries, in cooperation with government agencies, could offer training in new fields, e. g., renewable energy, digital, and sustainable technologies. Educational systems with 'world-class' status are likely to improve staff capabilities in mastering complex problems in an ever-changing world. Tunisia is already an important centre for knowledge and industry. Further responsive and proactive approaches will enhance its intellectual and innovative industry capabilities.

The ever-changing cross-section of education and knowledge economy in Tunisia makes clear that investment in people is as important a tool for development as it is a pillar of added-value social welfare. By fostering an education system that is research-led, Tunisia will harness the power of education for private and capital productivity to transform itself into a dominant international player.

Security Concerns and International Relations

Current security issues as well as international relations remain instrumental in Tunisia's development. The new era in Tunisian democracy, since the Arab revolution, has been accompanied by an array of new challenges, particularly those of security with internal and external roots. The border domain has identified terrorism-related issues, complex criminal systems, and border control as its primary development challenges.

From an external viewpoint, Tunisia is characterised by an unpredictable and volatile geopolitical landscape, compounded by intrastate conflicts, shifting migration patterns, and the ever-evolving interplay of global powers. Tunisia's national security structures and systems have been profoundly altered since the onset of the aforementioned challenges. These changes have been the result of attempts to reshape the security environment through the radical transformation of security apparatuses, the enhancement of border security, and anti-radicalisation strategies. Tunisia's collaborative endeavours with bordering countries, global partners, and conglomerate associations to tackle mutual security problems underscore the cooperative nature of the challenges faced. Tunisia's participation in the Global Counterterrorism Forum and cooperation in initiatives with the EU has proactively attempted to reinforce its security and defence posture while also integrating its national efforts into the regional and global security framework. In addition to this, Tunisia has adopted a fusion of distinct and divergent foreign policies with a more expansive view of Tunisia's international role. Tunisia's position between the Arab and European worlds has enabled the country to evolve a more realistic foreign policy, capitalising on its geographical position for economic and diplomatic pursuits. It also maintains an active foreign policy with regional institutions such as the Arab League and the African Union, and has been active in the region's security and conflict resolution efforts.

Moreover, this country also has friendly relations with the major powers of the world and is active in the multilateral system regarding the global south's common peace, security, and sustainable development goals.

Tunisia's permanence and national interests are central to its foreign negotiations and will remain critical in the future. Trade cooperation and development initiatives shore up Tunisia's regime development against terrorism and other governance threats in its foreign policy portfolio. Growing Tunisia's economy helps enhance the regime's resilience against terrorism and associated crime. Developments in foreign relations will shape Tunisia's international stance as its security policy evolves. Tunisia's foreign relations strategy will focus on promoting international bilateral and multilateral agreements grounded in international law, as well as achieving peace and security agreements to address global gaps in these areas. Tunisia will continue to pursue its national security agenda and foster relations to build coalitions for global security issues in the region. Tunisia will continue to strive to contribute to the region's diplomacy and peace.

Civic Engagement and Democratic Participation

The practice of civic engagement and its active democratic aspect are the foundational elements of any vigilant and dynamic society. As Tunisia prepares to respond to its contemporaneous challenges, these aspects gain further significance. It is essential for citizens to actively partake and engage in discussions for the desired development and inclusivity of the nation. Democratic participation is more than the right to vote; rather, it encompasses the participation and engagement of individuals and groups in civil society, advocacy, and public discourse. At the primary level, civic responsibility entails a commitment to social integration and cohesion. It is a shared responsibility of the citizens to collectively resolve problems and assist in the development of the country. In addition, the enhancement of self-governance in society, nurtured within the much-needed accountability and transparency in the administrative setup, encourages citizens to partake and actively engage in the formulation of policies as well as in the behavioural standards of the institutions and public organisations. This is all the more reason why a comprehensive structure for promoting civic awareness is important in Tunisia. Tunisia's various segments of society nurture civic learning and public discourse as effective means of advancing political participation and civic engagement.

This approach supports democratic principles while fostering greater awareness about rights, responsibilities, and mechanisms of participatory governance. Furthermore, digital tools for civic engagement can help enhance and broaden participation to more people. Investing in technology to improve information access, e-governance, and civic interaction can help overcome distance-related participation hurdles and enhance the scope and depth of representation in governance. Supporting marginalised groups and youth leaders as key components of civic engagement deepens the process of expanding participation. While Tunisia grapples with the socio-political constructs of the present, initiatives to deepen the scope of participation in democracy are of utmost importance. Fostering participatory democracy entails the active involvement of youth, women, ethnic minorities, and those marginalised in the democratic process through policy co-creation. Tunisia's efforts to achieve stability and growth must be anchored in the respect for fundamental freedoms, the protection of human rights, and the promotion of pluralism. Tunisia must harness its people's ability to define their future and their exceptionalism.

As the country progresses, its enduring commitment to civic engagement and democratic participation showcases the will and strength of civilisation.

Conclusion: Prospects for Stability and Growth

The stability and growth of Tunisia within the new contexts of socio-political engagement is a challenge in and of itself. Examining the case of Tunisia, the full engagement of the citizenry comes foremost in the democratic decision-making processes. This is the case primarily because if there is political stability, the robust participatory framework may empower the citizenry fully. This, in turn, enhances social stability and cohesion. Furthermore, active participation in the decision processes, even at the grassroots level, enhances the growth of the economy. If properly exploited, Tunisia's developing democracy will bring growth and stability through the active involvement of its citizens. However, citizen participation in Tunisia's democracy is primarily a form of political engagement. The economy outside politics and governance, however, remains the most decisive factor for growth and stability.

Tunisia, enhanced by its focus on global trade, investment, and innovation, can achieve economic resilience. With proactive steps taken to increase its external competitiveness, a diversified economy can sustain vibrancy and external shocks at the same time. This diverse economy, which is based on proactive investments in technology and digital infrastructure, will boost productivity and entrepreneurship. It will, thus, sustain economic growth. The process of urbanisation, along with certain social trends, suggests several positive fundamentals for economic growth. Urbanisation and social equilibrium have the potential to sustain and, thus, foster more prosperous communities in the country. Urban smart technologies, which facilitate optimum resource allocation, can strengthen societal resilience. This, in turn, enhances the effectiveness of public services. On the other hand, we need to balance growth with underlying environmental pressures. A focus on Tunisia's growth will expose the country and the wider global economy to certain renewable investments that are low-risk and, thus, economically sustainable. Such actions, combined with other green initiatives, will sustain the wellbeing of present and future generations. Education alongside the cultivation of a knowledge economy are the most important foundations for positive and sustained growth. Having an educated populace, with skills that are more sophisticated than what the local economy needs, will foster a system that nurtures innovation and growth.

Analysing global trends and investing in quality education and research can ensure long-term prosperity for Tunisia. Tunisia can engage with global and regional stakeholders in ways that enhance cooperation, develop diplomacy, and improve strategic partnerships. Tunisia aims to foster a zone of peace that maximises sustainable development and growth while nurturing proactive approaches to national security, particularly through collaborative initiatives. Tunisia faces complex problems but is proactively pursuing growth and stability. These problems can be resolved through a strategy that combines proactive international outreach with a consolidated domestic framework built upon democracy, economic strength, social equity, technological progress, ecological sustainability, educational advancement, and globalised foreign policy. These pillars guarantee Tunisia's long-term growth and stability.

www.ingramcontent.com/pod-product-compliance
Lightning Source LLC
Chambersburg PA
CBHW020529080526
44583CB00013B/792